I0055429

#1 Bestselling Author

ELINOR MOSHE

LEADERSHIP
in
CONSTRUCTION

Principles of
Exceptional, Exemplary and Excellent
Industry Leadership

KMD
BOOKS

Copyright © Elinor Moshe

First published in Australia in 2022
by KMD Books
Waikiki, WA 6169

All rights reserved. No part of this book may be used or reproduced by any means, graphic, electronic, or mechanical, including photocopying, recording, taping or by any information storage retrieval system without the written permission of the copyright owner except in the case of brief quotations embodied in critical articles and reviews.

Because of the dynamic nature of the Internet, any web addresses or links contained in this book may have changed since publication and may no longer be vaild. The views expressed in this work are solely those of the author and do not necessarily reflect the views of the publisher and the publisher hereby disclaims any responsibility for them.

Cover design by Ida Jensson

Edited by Chelsea Wilcox

Typeset in Adobe Garamond Pro 12.5/18pt

A catalogue record for this work is available from the National Library of Australia

National Library of Australia Catalogue-in-Publication data:

Leadership in Construction/Elinor Moshe

ISBN:
978-0-6454076-6-2
(Paperback)

ISBN:
978-0-6454076-7-9
(Ebook)

In gratitude and appreciation to:
Every guest who said yes.
The exceptional leaders in my life:
Mum and Dad, Ron and Caroline.
Every constructor who chooses to listen to Constructing
You.

CONTENTS

INTRODUCTION

It all starts and ends with leadership.

Yet, right now, the construction industry and the world as a whole are experiencing a severe leadership crisis. How did it all end up like this?

According to a 2014 survey published by Deloitte University Press, the need for 'leaders at all levels' is one of the twelve critical issues identified in the Global Human Capital Trends. And this critical issue is being felt more deeply and dramatically now than ever before, as the construction industry enters new frontiers after being trialled and tested during 'unprecedented times'. Whether you are onboard or not, we're seeing a large readjustment and leadership evolution. Disruption is knocking at our door as the industry has been suffocated from it for a very long time.

Despite the advancements in technology, theories and methodologies, products and building materials, and new software as a service (SaaS), there is one function that any sort of artificial intelligence or manufacturing trend cannot replace – the heart, mind and soul of an exceptional leader. The sheer necessity and unique ability of an exemplary, exceptional and excellent leader to band organisations, communities and the masses together under a uniting, progressive and inspiring vision can only be undertaken by a person. What it takes – to bring people along with you, to stand up for a cause, to be an agent of change, to inspire the hearts and minds of those who choose to follow you – is not just an art and a science, but a privilege. An honour earnt by an individual, and a duty that is not taken lightly. And precisely what the construction industry needs.

For it is only exemplary leadership now, which is a total rejection of mediocrity which has permeated every crevice, that will project the industry forward and create structural shifts in the aged, conservative and traditional industry that is construction. It is only those with enough fire in their heart and backbone to stand up for what they believe to construct an alternative future in the industry which will bring in fresh air and perspective against the age-old 'we've always done it this way'.

This book has been constructed to provide you with real-time lessons, principles and insights straight from the construction industry to feed the ambitions and aspirations of those with the fire of leadership within them. So you, too, can be an exceptional, exemplary and excellent leader held to the highest standards. To do that, I bring to you a marriage of insights and principles from the Thought Leadership model of leadership and traditional leadership, along with the invaluable contributions of some of the other exceptional leaders in the industry, who to date have displayed the utmost representation and character of brilliant leadership.

It is my duty as an industry leader to demonstrate that leadership is a function and what is possible as an industry leader – not tied to title, but to being and serving – and how possible it is for you to step into that at whatever stage you are in your career. Leadership starts with rejecting what is, adjusting how you see the world, who you decide to be and how you wish to serve.

It is a pleasure and privilege to introduce the nine exemplary leaders and industry titans in the construction industry and cognate disciplines who have generously provided their insights, principles and wisdom on my podcast, *Constructing You*, and now in this book:

- Alison Mirams – Chief Executive Officer of Roberts Co
- David Russo – Principal, Victoria and Board Member of Johnstaff
- Davina Rooney – Chief Executive Officer of Green Building Council of Australia
- George Abraham – Managing Director of Hickory
- Mark Nathan – Managing Director of Neoscape
- Melanie Kurzydlo – Director of Strategy and Business Relations of Growthbuilt
- Rami Adra – Director of Mossman Builders
- Sarah Slattery – Managing Director of Slattery
- Tooey Courtemanche – Founder, President and CEO of Procore Technologies

Whilst leadership principles and lessons are broad and wide, those contained hereon have been kept congruent and succinct to those shared by the contributors and teamed with my own experiences. This ensures that everything contained in this book is based on real-life experiences that have already been translated into real-life results, and not rote theory that hasn't been tried and tested.

While you'll never stop developing yourself should you wish to rise to a leadership position, I will provide you with the most imperative insights, principles and lessons that will allow you to experience the greatest leaps towards achieving leadership status and recognition. Wouldn't you like to cut through the theory and learn from real-time experience that will enable you to make the greatest difference in your life and that of others?

This book is written for the ambitious and driven future and current leaders in the industry, who:

- Are not willing to take any shortcuts in their development to function as a leader.
- Have a burning desire and passion within to cause some necessary disruption.
- Do not accept average or mediocre standards and hold themselves to the highest regard and standard.
- Are focused on how they can constantly serve and add values to others first, without expecting anything in return.
- Are willing to earn the right to lead.

I wrote this book for you to guide, inspire and direct you to achieve one of the most revered, desired and important functions of society – that of a leader. I will be direct with you, challenge you and get you to think far beyond the superficial and surface-level thinking in order to become excellent. I have openly shared lessons with you from my own leadership journey, because under no means am I sugar-coating the friction and growth required to become a leader. If it was a walk in the park, everyone would do it. It's anything but. You certainly don't have to agree with everything, for I'm not a leader who seeks consensus. But before you reject or neglect an idea, think about it.

Let's go on this journey to construct you as an exceptional, exemplary and excellent industry leader together – you ready?

Let's go.

***

AUTHOR'S NOTE

The views, perspectives and writings in this book are my own, unless where a direct quotation or a summation or reference to a third party is made. Any opinions, experiences and insights shared by me are also my own and do not reflect that of the contributors. The biography and company of all contributors is correct at the time of publishing.

MY CONTINUED JOURNEY

My first book, *Constructing Your Career*, served as volume one to my own career. It's the guidebook that allowed me to have an identifiable successful career in the construction industry and one which was always in me to write. But I am open about my journey and the moments, decisions and actions which continue to lead me to where I am today, for it didn't end there. I can continuously trace back to the tipping points and pivotal moments in retrospect which led me down the path of Thought Leadership, and what I wish to openly share with you. In ambition to guide, inspire and direct you to see that where you are today is not a reflection of your entire future. There's always more.

I have always been one to have multiple things on the go in my life. Whether it be a side hustle, volunteering or generating projects for myself, there has always been something outside of the 'seven to five' and a new massive goal that needs to be met. It always felt natural to me to have multiple career paths. Why be one-dimensional in your career approach? A formative failure on my journey to seeking more was collaborating with two other people in industry to deliver workshops and events for the industry, as we were doing that at the time under a professional capacity for a not-for-profit and thought, *Why not try a hand at it ourselves?* And this opened up a whole new world for me. A world of creation, ideation, servitude, marketing, social media, community building, speaking, content creation – the list goes on. It was the initial spark that opened my world view over and above thinking that a career was just about what happens between an employer and employee, or that I constantly needed to be under someone else's brand to deliver value. I realised I could create a vehicle on my own terms and merits.

It was due to this side hustle that I went to a networking event. The speaker at the time asked a very simple question – 'What are your top four values?' I couldn't answer. I had no idea. Integrity? Honesty? This stung me. How could I not know? (It's a universal rule – anything that you don't spend time figuring out, won't be figured out.) So I turned to my journalling practice to start asking myself what were then seemingly difficult questions. I started my journalling practice as a space to work out (then) difficult decisions. I loved construction and working on project delivery, but I also loved this other world of creating, producing, relationship building, mentoring, the prospect of building a business from the ground up, and the opportunities it could afford when done with intense structural integrity. There was this dance I was doing in my journal, where I couldn't figure out how to marry construction with other areas that were bringing me fulfilment – speaking, mentoring, creating, time freedom. Journalling was my outlet to have a very deep introspection with myself, questioning why I was doing what I was doing. Slowly but surely, cracks in my old paradigm started to appear. Not that I was able to recognise it back then, as a paradigm shift.

This discourse within me carried on for nine months, during which I invested a lot of time on myself. I had moments where I worked my way into a total state of anxiety because everything I thought I knew and thought I wanted was not aligned with my new vision anymore. I frequently get asked – 'How did your vision come about?' It was through the journalling practice of spending a lot of time with my thoughts and without judgement, putting on the page what in my heart of hearts I truly desired. Of course, at the time, I had zero idea as to how that would come into fruition. But, with a captivating and compelling vision and enough self-belief and belief that the conceived vision can meet your reality, will the universe align the right people and opportunities to make that happen. You'll see precisely how, shortly.

I turned to my mentor at the time, where I tried to describe this inner conflict between the limitations of working for an employer versus my vision and my new-found realisations of the opportunities out there. All of a sudden, just having a corporate career felt suffocating. I specifically remember this grey, bleak, still October morning in 2018 where I tried articulating this inner conflict and pull towards something outside of a regular career path. All I got was a mocked response of, 'Well if that's what you're feeling you should just go be an entrepreneur straight away.' It was mentioned in judgement, as if this world of creating something out of nothing wasn't available to me. Only to others. Holding the opinion of my expired mentor above mine, I quelled my ambitions and resigned to just keep on doing what I was doing. I remember that dull, grey Melbourne day standing in the site shed staring at crushed rock after that phone call, looking out the shed window with security bars, reflecting the mental prison that I felt I was in. And I just thought, *This can't be it.*

I left it at that, not speaking of my ambitions and dreams further, and for the next six months, residing to feeling lost, confused and diminished. That was exemplified when fractures in the side hustle were showing, because my natural disposition is to stand out, but that wasn't working for others. So, I continued to recede and suppress my authentic state of being – well, now what I know is my authentic state and my prerogative. I went day by day with a constant friction and frustration, trying to look at my career as an entity. A business within itself that will be in operation for at least another four decades – what was I trying to make of it? I was deeply conflicted because I had arrived at a destination in my career that I so fervently thought I wanted, and I was deeply dissatisfied. Again – I knew there was more, I just didn't have a clue what it could look like. I vehemently couldn't imagine projecting where I was then, over the entirety of my career (drastic, but accurate). It just didn't align, it didn't make sense, and to my core I knew something was missing.

At the same time, two events happened. One, I found the marriage between construction and mentoring, which was the start of my business, Australia's first construction coach: The Construction Coach. It was February 2019 when my tutoring pipeline dried up as the listing platform changed their listing services and immediately all clients were gone. My initial thought was – *If I am relying on a third party for clients, I am always going to be at their behest. They control my income and reach.* I thought, *How can I reach more people on my own?* I journalled, again about trying to find the vehicle that would marry two passions. April 2019 came along, and it was the prolonged industry shutdown that finally gave me space to think. I was working on an extremely dissatisfying project, in which the misaligned people and projects were negatively seeping and draining other areas of my life. The time away from the place which was a mental prison was welcomed. On the Wednesday of the break, I lay awake at 11pm, and I got the download – the name – *The Construction Coach.* I was up till 5am registering a domain, ABN and filling a notebook with ideas as to what The Construction Coach is, could be and how it can serve the industry. I was electric. This was it. This would be my vehicle. I spent one month in doubt and action, putting an announcement on LinkedIn with my elementary website announcing my new venture on 5 May 2019.

The second formative event was my then-mentor starting a construction company, and so badly wanting me to work with him. It wasn't the issue of working for a startup that didn't allow me to make the decision to move. There was nothing fulfilling to me about the proposal, but I couldn't articulate why. I couldn't give a clear answer as to why I didn't want to move. There was the option of 'one day' being an equity partner, and when I delved into that, responses were along the lines of it being a twenty-year play and subject to other partners simply liking me more than others they bring into the business. This simply didn't make sense to me. To dedicate two decades of my life building someone else's vision on promises with no foundations? Don't be mistaken, I'm not adverse to trusting the process, working very hard and sacrificing what I need to, nor do I have a sense of entitlement that anything worth having is to be handed to me on a silver platter. But to sacrifice my most valuable asset of time to do this for someone else wasn't sitting right. The conversations about the 'opportunity' got deeper and eventually I owned up in not so many words that I was pulled towards my own business, and I needed to give my own vision and ambitions a priority. The mentoring relationship ended there abruptly, and how grateful I am it did. I learnt two important lessons with this event. One, is that opportunity is a perception. What one person perceives as opportunity is not necessarily that for others. But to know this, you need to have your own vision. And two, no matter how important you thought people were in your life, they need to leave, so as to make space for aligned people from your future. Some people will be around for a reason, a season or a lifetime.

Without a mentor, but with a vision that I didn't know how to make meet reality, a side hustle that was on its last straws and now having a blog and a dedicated Instagram page that I had little idea what to do with, I knew I needed to start upskilling myself and start identifying what I didn't even know about starting a business – marketing, blogging – clients? I knew that I didn't know a lot, and I certainly didn't have the ego to think that I'd figure it all out myself.

Prior to setting out on the Thought Leadership path, I was a frequent enough user on LinkedIn. I didn't know the first thing about real LinkedIn marketing, branding, positioning or adding value, other than it was a brilliant platform to reach a segment of the audience in the industry. I got a message on LinkedIn from a coach that she was hosting an event in Docklands about using LinkedIn for business. How perfectly aligned – I bought a ticket immediately as I had heard of two people on the panel, and the other two seemed worthy of listening to. One of the other two was Ron Malhotra.

There is a time in my life before Ron, wherein retrospect is viewed by me in greyscale and slow motion. Then there is the time after Ron, which is magnified and viewed in high-speed and technicolour. A hyperreality of dreams, ambitions and achievements. I passionately and openly speak about the mentoring experience and the immense gratitude I have for Ron. Until the end of time, I am gratefully with every corner of my mind, heart and soul to have met Ron on 16 June 2019. I'm very sentimental with these turning points in my life. It makes for a great story. I remember going into that event and having Ron greet me at the door. I was so intimidated that I couldn't even look him in the eye, and quickly brushed myself off to take a seat. This, of course, isn't a reflection of Ron. It was a reflection of me – that I had handed over my power, my control and my presence, lowering it to a point where I didn't want to be seen or heard, expressing nothing because I thought it made other people feel uncomfortable and intimidated. At that point, I'd just about lost myself to become just another face in the crowd. Hell will have to freeze over before I even consider making that dire mistake again. There are few people that you will ever meet who so quickly pierce through to you. To date, I remember so much of what Ron contributed to that panel event that night, because in a room of sixty people, I felt that he was talking straight to me. *Who is this person? Who is this person dressed impeccably in a three-piece suit, so powerful, so whole?* At the end of the event there was an opportunity to talk to Ron, and like lightning speed I went up there. His business partner remembers me on that day so well, how I just went up to her and knew exactly what I wanted. I still had a little bit of backbone left after giving so much away to others.

I got on a call with Ron, and assuredly, the first ninety minutes I ever spoke to Ron blew my mind. Ron saw something in me which I didn't see, which I *couldn't* see. As I'm writing, I'm tearing up, because one of the most heartwarming and moving experiences that you can have is for someone to see you. Not just for what you are today, but for all of who you can be. I'm emotional at the thought of what would have been had Ron not extended his belief in me, even when I had very little left in me. Our conversation centred around The Construction Coach and what's important to me. I found myself being very open with Ron, which also took me by surprise. As I had become wary of sharing my vision and ambition so as to not be discounted, and on the whole, I had done a great job in my twenties suppressing emotion and expression in order to go unnoticed. And then entered the Thought Leadership world. I've never heard this term before. In no book, in no podcasts, in no articles on business, careers, education. It was the first time such a world presented itself to me. Did it seem too good to be true? A world that was different to traditional employment and traditional entrepreneurship? A world that was based about my message and philosophies, because what I have to say matters? A world where recognition, adding value to others and eventually commercialising this was available? A world that looked like an even more perfect marriage of what I was being drawn towards? Was this actually possible? I was presented with the option to go down it, and to go away and think about it.

For a year up until I got on the call with Ron, I was listening to podcasts about wealth and business. Listening to how others came up from nothing, rolled the dice on a mentor, and ten out of ten times they always said it was the best decision they ever made in their lives – certainly sticks with you. Our call was on a Thursday, so I had the weekend to think about it. Over the weekend, I laid in bed with a cold, reading *Secrets of the Millionaire Mind* by T Harv Eker. Up until this point, I hadn't invested in a mentor or a coach. No-one spoke to me. No-one had a pathway that was drawing me forward. No-one in my world then had the life and lifestyle and the results that I wanted. Except Ron. Of course, I turned to the journal, putting pen on paper as I still do every time I need to make a big decision. Choosing to roll the dice on the Thought Leadership pathway with Ron would have been the largest decision and investment I had to make in myself. Before writing this part of the book, I went to find my journal entry. It's confronting but also extremely special re-reading a journal entry, as it's such an intimate reflection between where you are now to your thoughts and feelings then. But I did write: *What if I don't do it?* This is why my former mentor had to leave my life, so as to not block or have agency over me, as I know the outcome of my decision would have been different.

Monday afternoon, I sent Ron a message asking if I would be supported on the journey, to which of course I got a yes, and I sent a response saying, *Okay, I'm in.* And that was that.

I still felt diminished, dismayed and extremely discontented with where I was in my career. But I knew that it couldn't stay that way. Nothing changes if nothing changes, and to have unconventional results, you need to take unconventional, immediate and massive action. Exactly what I did. I had an elementary understanding of what it meant to lead myself first before I lead others. But I knew that I cannot expect other people to take actions that I myself haven't taken. Unfortunately, that is commonplace practice that doesn't fall under the behaviours and actions of exemplary leadership. I knew that time was my most important asset, and I can make money for the rest of my life, but I cannot make more time. If my ambitions meant spending a few years laying the foundations, deferring gratification and simply trusting the process, then that's what would be. I didn't know myself enough back then, but I did know enough that if I set my mind to something, I achieve it. I knew myself enough to go all-in, back myself and work with Ron. This is the best adult decision I have made in my life, and how my world changed on 3 August 2019.

In my first Thought Leadership session with Ron, I read him my one-page vision. It's the vision that was expanding inside my heart and mind, but until Ron requested it, I hadn't put it on one page. It took all the courage I had to share it with someone new, to be so open and trusting. And Ron's first response was *wow*, followed by the conviction in his words and confirmation that it will all happen. And I can assuredly say that a very high percentage of that vision has already taken place, and I've expanded it time and time again since then.

If it wasn't for sitting with my thoughts and vision, if it wasn't for making a bold move when presented with the path less travelled, and if it wasn't for that little bit of belief in myself and the belief that Ron had in me, I wouldn't get to be anywhere near writing this book for you. There is no leadership without first leading yourself. Such opportunities that are in total alignment and congruency to get people to where they want to go present themselves. Except it comes looking like work, sacrifice and mental energy, which is why very few people in the world take it. What do most people think the start of leadership looks like? Comfort? Following the herd? Anything but. Most people operate out of a modality of lack and continue to make decisions based on this. When I made the decision to be mentored by Ron, it was made from a place of where I wanted to be, not where I was that day. I know now, with every ounce of my spirit and soul, that I was born to be a Thought Leader. I was given the mind, voice and prerogative to step into this world as one.

There is no experience akin to working with Ron Malhotra, who is larger than life. Each session shifted and clarified my philosophy and world view. Each session afforded me the most detailed, intricate and holistic ability to construct myself first, from the inside out. At the back of each session with Ron, I would wake up between 3-5am with a freight train of thoughts going through my mind, to the extent that I put a notebook next to my bed to capture the new thoughts and revelations, and started the days feeling electrified and supercharged. I found my passion, I found my purpose and I found my *why*. I came alive. This is significantly easier to do when you have a person who so deeply cares, like Ron. But everything that I thought I knew came crashing down. I spent months upon months in friction and running straight into the discomfort of growth – that is where I choose to live.

The journey continued. Public speaking, to me, happens as naturally as breathing. Ron recognised that my voice and speaking ability is a natural talent, and podcasting is a natural fit. It was coming through in my messaging, and what I am passionate about – that it's the people behind the projects which matter to me. I never saw myself as talking about the technical, conventional and recognised aspects of construction. I certainly can, as that's what my technical training has afforded me. But no-one was focusing on the people. No-one in the local industry – here, anyway – was turning inwards looking first at the individual and creating transformation and disruption from the inside out. Going through the mentoring experience with Ron, I was getting intimately familiar with the hidden, yet extremely powerful, determinants of career and life success, and assuredly, it has very minimal weighting on the technical skills, which are so commonly and incorrectly touted as the factors contributing to recognisable career success in the industry. Do you think people wanted to hear this, to start with? Absolutely not. A desktop research of podcasts at the time revealed that there were forty-six podcasts about construction – the majority associated with the technical know-how, or were redundant with no new episodes in the last few years. But none focused on the people. I sat with this glaring omission in the marketplace, thinking about what I could do to add value to it. I needed a microphone – immediately.

In October 2019 I came up with the name, *Constructing You,* where I would share the stories of the people behind the projects. In December 2019 I held my breath as I pressed send to the first ten people I approached. It was electrifying receiving the first yes, second yes, third yes. I've never interviewed another soul on this world before, let alone put it out there for anyone, anywhere, to listen, but I was doing this. I spent my jetlag hours in Israel at the start of 2020 devising questions for my guests, knowing that I didn't want to focus on publicly available information, but rather get into their person. Who did they have to become to achieve what they have? I walked into the office of my first guest two days after I landed, brand-new microphone in hand and ready to press record.

Like any entrepreneurial venture, you build it not knowing what the response will be. Especially when it's a first, and when you're still building your authority and cementing your position in your micro-niche. I knew from the outset this wouldn't be your average podcast, so I needed a unique way to launch. If I'm going to do something, I'm going to see it through and do whatever I have to in the process to give it every chance of success. So, I got a videographer and a drone, and launched *Constructing You* on 15 March 2020. In alignment with the fateful lockdown that became part of our lives.

The podcast was also inspired from my duty as an industry leader to show you what is possible. When I was going through university and expanding my networks in the formative days of my career, only a very narrow bandwidth of career options were presented – project manager, possibly a construction manager. The upper echelon positions, albeit a founder of a business or executive manager, were seemingly reserved for 'someone else', but not me. To realise that this is all possible for me, took years of mindset conditioning and development, as I've shared. It took time to develop vision and lift the ceiling on what can actually be achieved. Yet it still wasn't clear how to actually get 'there'. I asked the question, *What does it really take to have an exemplary career in property and construction today?* And, *Who do you have to become to achieve what you want?* Which lead to the conception of my podcast, *Constructing You.*

Constructing You shares the stories of the people behind the projects. The construction and property industries are people industries, after all. It still amazes me how some companies don't even profile the people within the organisation on their website, just the projects. Which adds to the fact that typically when we look at our built environment, and ask, *Who built this?* the answer is a name of a company. But who are the people behind the projects? Who are the ones who have vision and have brought them to life? That's why I started at the top and shared interviews with exemplary leaders and industry titans. It leans into the old adage, *You can't be what you can't see,* and how right that is. But I didn't only want to find out what they do, but also who they are and who they've had to become to achieve what they have, which has wholly been a publicly unavailable insight to the industry. It gives my listeners the insight to see who you need to become in order to achieve massive career and business success.

After interviewing over seventy exemplary leaders and industry titans (at the time of writing), predominantly in the construction, property and project management space, and in total alignment to the ethos of the podcast, I saw recurring themes. There are recurrences in the mindset and decisions that recognised industry leaders have made along their own journey to get them to where they are today. We don't all start off with equal resources, but we all have the same access to resourcefulness and to dictate our thinking to inform our behaviours and actions to get the results that we desire to see in our lives. I discovered this for myself, which is why I wanted to share my own journey with you first. These are leaders who have and are achieving exceptional results and outcomes for the construction industry. These are the people who understand that first they lead themselves, before they lead others. These are the people who have moved past convention, taken risks, and triumphed against professional and personal challenges. They're successful in their own right but recognised their value to the industry and constructing better futures than what currently is.

To give leaders and ambitious industry professionals a guide as to how, too, they can become exceptional, excellent and exemplary leaders in the construction industry serves as the purpose and motivation behind my writing on this book. Let's go behind the scenes of leadership. Because with the issues, afflictions and considerations in the construction industry, one thing I can see is necessary: exemplary leadership to shape the industry into the true potential that it can afford to those who work in it. And a total rejection of mediocrity which has been the standard too many have walked by and accepted for too long.

As a leader, one of the greatest impacts we can have is to contribute to the development of other leaders. My mission cannot be completed alone. I need the best of the best to rise up and take charge as well. And I truly hope that this book will contribute to your journey of stepping into your power, presence and being the vehicle of disruption and change, the fresh air that the industry needs, and attain the progression and recognition that you truly deserve. So you, too, are an exemplary leader and industry titan behind the projects.

HOW TO USE THIS BOOK

The chapters under each part have been divided to allow you to read the book sequentially, but also to come back to it as a reference as you progress along your journey. To be a 'Triple E' leader – exceptional, exemplary and excellent leader – in construction, requires you to build your leadership value on three pillars. A stool with three legs will not stand up if one leg is missing, and the same goes for the three arenas on which this book is constructed. Throughout this book, a leader who is considered as an exceptional, exemplary and excellent leader will be referred to as a Triple E leader for concision.

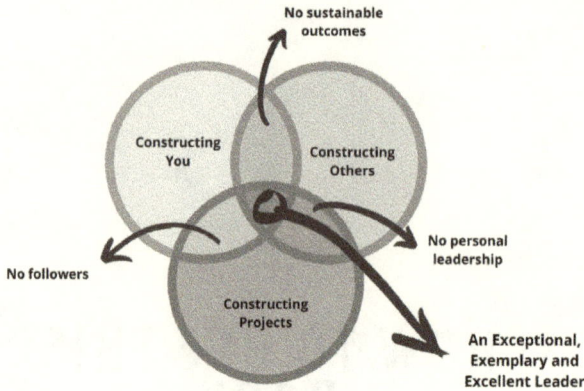

The Leadership in Construction Paradox™

If you work on constructing you and constructing others, that's great to an extent but it may exclude a focus on commercial outcomes and business performance. We can't have people feeling all inspired and fluffy on the inside and not driving commercial objectives. Your marker as a leader is a reflection of the results and value you deliver. As a leader, you're responsible for outcomes.

If you elect to work on yourself, and only focus on project outcomes without your people, then you are a lone wolf. A leader without followers is not a leader. If no-one is inspired and guided to go where you are going, then by the basic definition of leadership, that won't be you. You may achieve project or corporate outcomes, but that also cannot be at the expense of someone else being worse off after they have worked with you. Projects hereon will be a reference to both construction projects and a business as a whole entity and vice versa.

But if you only construct others and have your project outcomes in mind, then you are a great manager (possibly not even that, if you haven't spent any time developing yourself).

Management is not leadership. And if you cannot lead yourself, then you certainly cannot lead others. It is this forgotten pillar that makes or breaks one's pursuit of being a Triple E leader.

The sweet spot is in the middle. It's where all works under construction align reflecting your brilliant leadership ability. This doesn't happen overnight, over a month and not even a year. It happens over a lifetime, because being a leader inhabits each aspect of your life.

Whilst there are varying degrees of leadership capability, those who are ambitious at heart and driven to serve can only be aiming at the highest echelon of leadership. Per the Triple E Leadership Pyramid, there is less competition at the top, and also from where you can generate the greatest impact. It's the place of greatest inspiration to others, as you do truly have to consider who you have to become first, all the turbulence you need to go through, to get to the highest form of leadership. It's always your decision to what you will strive for and if you will take the road less travelled. The top of the pyramid is where there is the least competition, affording you more recognition, remuneration and progression than any other tier.

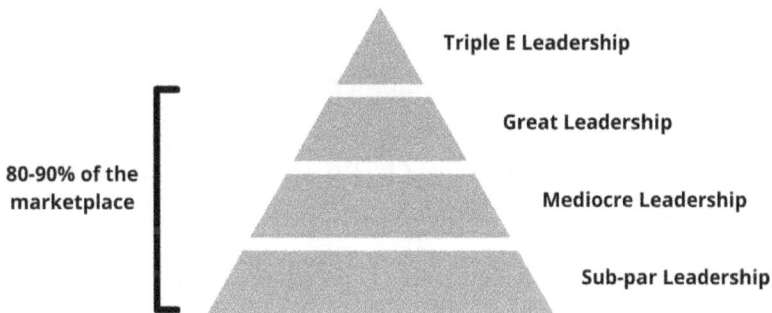

Triple E Leadership

Great Leadership

80-90% of the marketplace

Mediocre Leadership

Sub-par Leadership

The Triple E Leadership Pyramid ™

MEET THE EXEMPLARS

It's a pleasure and a privilege to bring the vision of this book to life in contribution with these nine exemplary leaders and industry titans. Their insights, principles and wisdom come from decades of trials and tribulations, venturing into the unknown, and in some cases, going where no other leader has gone before. This is the baseline of Triple E leadership, that if not generously shared would've taken many years for others to learn via trial and error. Their time and effort to be part of this book is met with deep appreciation, so let's meet them. In alphabetical order:

ALISON MIRAMS, CHIEF EXECUTIVE OFFICER OF ROBERTS CO

Alison Mirams is the founding chief executive officer of boutique tier one construction company Roberts Co. The company was founded in January 2017 and within the first three years has a workbook of over $1 billion. She is deeply passionate about addressing the systemic issues that exist in the construction industry and attracting and retaining more women in the industry.

Alison has worked in the construction industry for twenty-five years. Prior to establishing Roberts Co, Alison led the NSW/ACT regional business unit for Lendlease's Building business for nearly three years. Prior to joining Lendlease, she enjoyed a successful sixteen-year career at Multiplex, rising from contracts administrator to regional director.

Alison is a director of the UNSW foundation board, is a member of the TAFE commission advisory board and AeroPM advisory board. Alison was previously a director of the Australian Steel Institute and a member of the board of advisors for the Property Industry Foundation.

Alison received the Laing O'Rourke Business Woman of the Year award at the 2018 NAWIC (National Association of Women in Construction) NSW Awards for Excellence.

Alison holds a Bachelor of Building (Construction Economics) and a Graduate Diploma Urban Estate Management from UTS.

DAVID RUSSO, PRINCIPAL, VICTORIA AND BOARD MEMBER OF JOHNSTAFF

David has been a leader within the Victorian Johnstaff team for over ten years, as principal since 2013 and joined the National Board of Directors in November 2016. David has extensive experience managing and delivering a wide range of capital projects for clients in the public and private sectors, many of which have been complex projects in a variety of industries. His vast experience spans across health, aged care and complex education and research projects. The success of these projects has been built on collaboratively working with clients, having a strong team approach, and providing clients with excellent, transparent and honest communication. He deeply values the many relationships that he has developed over the past twenty years with industry leaders.

David is focused on ensuring that Johnstaff continues to support and guide strong relationships with clients. He has been influencing this through the ongoing development of Johnstaff's people and systems across all offices, so that Johnstaff's service offering is seamless to our clients, wherever their projects are being delivered.

David holds a Bachelor of Civil Engineering (Hons) and Bachelor of Commerce from the University of Melbourne, is a nationally recognised member of Engineers Australia and a graduate of the Australian Institute of Company Directors.

DAVINA ROONEY, CHIEF EXECUTIVE OFFICER OF GREEN BUILDING COUNCIL OF AUSTRALIA

A property professional with a passion for sustainability, Davina has led the Green Building Council of Australia since 2019. As a qualified engineer, she worked on large-scale construction projects in Sydney and London, and spent nearly a year building an award-winning school in the Himalayas.

She devoted a decade to driving sustainability at one of Australia's largest diversified property companies, Stockland, which culminated in Stockland's recognition as the world's most sustainable property company. Now leading a member organisation with 550-plus members with a combined value of $46 billion, Davina brings together practical knowledge, on-the-ground experience and a systematic approach to champion leadership in sustainable design and construction. She works with government and industry to advocate for supportive policy and transform complex supply chains.

Building on a strong legacy of leadership, Davina is elevating the GBCA's reach and impact into new markets. The property industry has recognised her leadership with multiple awards, including from the Property Council of Australia (PCA) and the National Association of Women in Construction.

GEORGE ABRAHAM, MANAGING DIRECTOR OF HICKORY

George Abraham is an established and respected leader within the construction industry, with a track record for delivering major complex projects. As managing director, he oversees Hickory operations and projects currently under contract worth over $1 billion.

With previous experience as a project and construction manager working directly with key stakeholders and clients, George maintains a positive, hands-on approach in his role to ensure construction projects are delivered to the highest standards. As a champion of quality and safety, he continually strives to raise industry standards and set new benchmarks in Australian construction on time, cost and quality.

In 2019, he proudly accepted the Council on Tall Buildings and Urban Habitat Award on behalf of Hickory for Construction Excellence, recognising projects that have made extraordinary contributions to the advancement of construction in tall buildings.

He fosters an inclusive and collaborative culture at Hickory, leading teams to achieve outstanding results. He inspires action by sharing his knowledge and experience, with a natural ability to empower and unlock potential in others.

Having previously worked for tier one construction companies, including Brookfield Multiplex and Baulderstone Hornibrook, George's career has been on an upward trajectory since graduating with first class honours from a construction management degree.

Recognised for his strong leadership skills, stakeholder management and knowledge of industrial relations, he quickly rose to prominence in the industry and is now set to lead Hickory's future success.

MARK NATHAN, MANAGING DIRECTOR OF NEOSCAPE

Mark is well regarded for his leadership capabilities, his ability to form and lead strong, dynamic project teams, and his enviable reputation for the delivery of successful, award-winning projects earned through thirty years of experience in the construction and property industry.

Mark founded Neoscape in 2013, with fellow director Darren Woolf, to provide the benefit of their extensive experience in project delivery and construction and a solution-focused approach to the property industry in the delivery of development management, project management and advisory services.

Prior to founding Neoscape, Mark enjoyed a career spanning over twenty-two years at tier one contractor Probuild. He established Probuild's Sydney office and was appointed their executive group in 2002. He became a minority shareholder in Probuild in 2005.

Throughout his career, Mark has been responsible for the successful procurement and delivery of a number of major national and award-winning projects which has earned him a reputation for integrity, commitment and professionalism throughout the property industry.

Mark is an MGSM, MBA graduate, an Unlimited Registered Building Practitioner with the Building Practitioners Board, Victoria, and an Unlimited Licensed Contractor with the Department of Fair Trading, New South Wales.

MELANIE KURZYDLO, DIRECTOR STRATEGY AND BUSINESS RELATION OF GROWTHBUILT

An experienced senior executive and business strategist with a creative flair for customising operational plans to align with market demands and company expansion goals, Melanie has led multidisciplinary teams driving new revenue streams to enhance profitability, whilst improving employee retention benchmarks linking purpose and passion for a powerful profitable outcome.

Currently as the director of strategy and business relations at Growthbuilt, holding a leading role on the executive leadership team, spearheads the company's growth, enterprise and business development strategy which has created an industry-leading contractor with revenue growth and heightened profitability year on year. Melanie transformed a one-dimensional residential builder into a multi-delivery integrated contractor by identifying and entering multiple private and government industry sectors. Her passion and drive to support organisations that align with her own is key to her success, currently sitting on multiple cross-industry boards and key industry steering committees driving diversity, progression and innovation within the development, construction, property industry and beyond.

She sits on the PCA Diversity Committee (since 2018), is a board member of CoreNet Global Australia (since 2018), a board member of the Giants (GWS) Foundation and a board member of the UNSW Foundation Board. She is also the co-lead of Building Pride, the leading LGBTI+ property group to raise awareness of related topics within the industry. A winner of the 2019 NAWIC Crystal Vision Award for the advancements of women and other diverse groups. She continually aims to assist in driving diverse and inclusive initiatives for the property development and construction industry in areas of women, LGBTI+, reconciliation, mental health, age and culture, and firmly believes progression and impactful change all starts and finishes with education.

RAMI ADRA, DIRECTOR OF MOSSMAN BUILDERS

Infused with entrepreneurial spirit, Rami is always asking *How can things be done better?* After running and selling a successful heating and cooling business, Rami became a registered building practitioner with qualifications in building and construction in order to build Mossman. His specialty is the back end; guiding Mossman to meet its ever-evolving challenges, finding new and better ways to benefit customers through the use of digital technology, and spending a lot of time with clients to ensure their every need is taken care of.

Success is Rami's only yardstick, and he enjoys nothing more than creating a great environment in which the Mossman team can work and succeed together.

SARAH SLATTERY, MANAGING DIRECTOR OF SLATTERY

Slattery is a property, infrastructure and construction advisory firm specialising in early phase advisory, quantity surveying and cost management.

Sarah brings more than thirty years' experience as a quantity surveyor in Australia and the UK, having worked across all sectors of the property industry. Managing director at Slattery since 2017, her in-depth knowledge of the field was fostered from a young age through exposure to her family's business and has been a way of life ever since.

Sarah has developed specialist skills in complex, design-oriented projects, namely in education, arts and culture, health and transport developments. She is a regular commentator on procurement, supply chains and market conditions. Her energy, expertise and passion for the industry has seen her become a trusted advisor to significant government, developer and private clients.

A director of TEN Women group, Sarah has been pivotal in furthering gender equality in the property industry. Passionate about mentoring, she has been a PCA mentor, deputy chair of the inaugural Women & Diversity Committee and a sponsor of the 500 Women initiative. She oversaw the implementation of Slattery's mentor program consolidating a supportive culture of development and continuous learning.

Sarah has significant involvement in the property industry and is currently a member of the construction forecasting council of the Australian Construction Industry Forum (ACIF), a development and funding committee member for Uniting Housing (VIC, TAS) and a member of the Siena College Strategic Property Committee. Sarah's insights have been shared in *The Australian,*

The Age, ABC News, as well as various ACIF, AIQS, CEDA and PCA forums.

TOOEY COURTEMANCHE, FOUNDER, PRESIDENT AND CEO OF PROCORE TECHNOLOGIES

Craig 'Tooey' Courtemanche is the founder, president and chief executive officer of Procore Technologies. Beginning his professional life as a builder, he has always been passionate about building things and straddled two worlds that felt disconnected: construction and technology.

Discovering the world of software in the 1990s, Tooey left his professional real estate developer career to immerse himself in the Silicon Valley tech boom. Working in San Francisco inspired him to found his first web startup which enabled Fortune 1000 companies to transition from analog to web services. It was here that he learned firsthand the impact digital transformation could have on different industries. In 2002, he brought his two passions, technology and construction, together and started Procore. He set out to build a company that connected everyone in construction on a global platform, and thus improved the lives of everyone in construction. He knew the best way to do this was to invest in culture from day one and has since created a culture of Procorians who have empathy for the industry they serve and thrive when they're onsite with customers, working alongside them to develop solutions to the challenges they face. Over 1.6 million owners, general contractors and specialty contractors across the globe use the Procore platform to do what they do best; build. In its nineteen years, Procore has won numerous awards for its products, culture and customer support.

PART ONE

CONSTRUCTING YOU

Constructing You is personal leadership. If you were expecting a tactical leadership book, I will have to disappoint. You have to lead yourself before you can lead others. That's why I shared an intimate and detailed window into my world prior to the one you see today – it was messy, chaotic, courageous and bold. I had to solve problems for myself first. There are all too many people who pre-qualify themselves to be a leader, but if you actually look behind the facade, you will not find anything remarkable, nor that they have done anything that is a stretch outside of their comfort zone. No-one wants to follow the leader when they know the leader can't succeed. That's why, as much as you desire to lead and inspire others, that's not a long-lasting possibility if you first don't demonstrate that you can generate success for yourself. You need to demonstrate that you can first climb a proverbial ladder before having others follow suit.

'Work on yourself before anything else, even before your business,' says Adra. 'Fix your mindset and work on your self-development. That's probably the best advice I could give anybody. Before you even consider [being a leader], write what kind of person you are and how you're going to deal with other people.'

If you cannot solve problems for yourself, and raise your own consciousness and standards, how do you expect to do that for others? Do you know what it really takes? You can only lead people from a higher consciousness than they are on; otherwise it is the equivalent of the blind leading the blind. Before I stepped into the leadership arena, I spent twelve months working on me with my mentor, Ron Malhotra. But even prior to this, I started unravelling and delving into the inner work that is first required to achieve success in my reality. It's this inner work which is hugely avoided. Before you can go out there and earn your position as a leader, or rise to it, you have to close the blinds to the outside world and undertake an introspection to expand and shift your own paradigms and deal with your own blind spots. And I still do this every day. Get your own house in order before you go into anyone else's. If you think that all you know right now is all that you need to know to lead, well, there's already a major flaw and blind spot.

Abraham remarks, 'You never stop learning about yourself and the adjustments that you need to make to make to yourself and your behaviours …' Your duty as a leader is to see what others cannot see, but you need to expand your own world view first. This brings us to the first leadership principle: your vision.

CHAPTER ONE

YOUR VISION

VISION

'Don't let others tell you what you can't do. Don't let the limitations of others limit your vision. If you can remove your self-doubt and believe in yourself, you can achieve what you never thought possible.' – **Roy T Bennett**

Conceiving a vision is truly one of the most beautiful things you can ever do for yourself. Yet the majority of people have fallen into societal conditioning and have lost the audacity to dream. Where along the conventional path that has been followed have you stopped to dream? When did you stop to remember your wildest ambitions, dreams and aspirations that you had as a child? Or even when you first entered into the industry? When did you stop letting your mind wander, dragging it back to a reality that wasn't even set by you in the first place? To think that the majority of people will leave this world never seeing their own vision, let alone experiencing it, is simply saddening. In discussion, someone asked me where you can find the largest repository of ideas. The cemetery. If you cannot cast a compelling vision for yourself and express foresight, then you won't be able to do this for others at any level. If you can't show someone more than what they can see today, it's not leadership.

Vision is defined as something that is, or has, been seen. The mere fact that you can have a glimpse into your future suggests that it's already done. It's been seen, therefore it exists. Think about anything that was ever constructed in the physical world. It was first constructed in the mental world. It had to be seen first. Isn't this precisely how building construction works? The same applies to your person.

Vision is also the ability to look into the future and conceive a reality that doesn't yet exist in the present time. As I shared with you in my journey, it was vision that changed the game. Not just for me, but for others. My vision is to construct exceptional futures for the people and businesses within the construction industry. An industry is a system, which is made up of the sum of its parts. What are the parts? The people. So, to construct the exceptional future of the industry, I have to start from the inside out – of the industry itself and of the people within. Imagine the construction industry future generations could have if every person worked first on the greatest project they'll ever get to work on. It would be a book in itself, itemising the benefits. My business, The Construction Coach, is therefore an extension of that vision. I mentor, coach and advise on anything but the technical side of the industry. I saw the vision for the business being a one-of-a-kind for the industry, and so it is. You will never hear me speak about pouring concrete. I had to create beyond what was already in existence in terms of mentoring and coaching for the industry. The larger the vision you have, you'll find that it's no longer about you, and it enables you to make it more about other people.

> *'Good business leaders create a vision, articulate the vision, passionately own the vision, and relentlessly drive it to completion.'* – **Jack Welch**

Not casting a compelling vision for yourself, or for others, is a leadership flaw, as it's a fundamental requisite of leadership. The translation of that vision to reality is the merit of a leader, as is being able to cast that vision far and wide and bring as many people as possible along with them. I've done hundreds of hours of consulting calls to date, and at least 80-90% of the time when I ask a prospect, *What do you want?* silence seeps into the conversation filled with blank stares. If you don't know where you, as an individual, are going, then where can you possibly lead others to? The same directionless venture, which is no more exceptional than the present reality? That's not inspiring at all. Most people simply do not have any foresight. Foresight is the ability to look into the future and marry the consequences of your actions today into how they will translate into the future. For example, if you don't invest your money today, it's guaranteed to be worth less in three years. If you don't invest in your mindset, skillset, soulset or heartset, you can ensure to continually arrive at destinations in your life unfulfilled and also live out your life on repeat. It's a simple rate of diminishing return. If you eat unhealthy foods and don't work out, you can ensure you'll be shopping for a new wardrobe soon. Yet, most people know the consequences and have a superficial level of understanding, but still undertake the same course of action. So vision and foresight is not common. And that's where there is immense opportunity to cast the vision – for yourself, and for others. Most people simply don't have the audacity to dream. Conditioning from a multitude of societal factors has eroded people's abilities to even wish or want something for themselves that falls outside the realm of their intellect or by looking in the rear-view mirror to construct the future. Have you ever wondered why that's the case?

'Leadership is lifting a person's vision to high sights, the raising of a person's performance to a higher standard, the building of a personality beyond its normal limitations.' –
Peter Drucker

Let's look at the founding story of Procore Technologies. Courtemanche was so passionate about this vision of connecting everyone on a global platform and to elevate the lives of everyone in construction. They started by selling software to people that didn't have the internet on a construction site. 'I grew up in construction, I ran a technology company and built a house. I brought all of that together having felt all the pain that most people feel during a highly uncoordinated construction process. As I was going through the process of building the home, it dawned on me that there were two elements that really weren't being accounted for – the personal element, all these amazing people, tradespeople that come together on a daily basis to work together, and the technology component, which was completely missing. There were a lot of legal pads, and frankly, fax machines back then. It dawned on me that we would be much more efficient and I would be a much happier homeowner if we connect all of the people with technology to ensure that they were able to work more efficiently. People using technology to connect are more effective than the chaos of just showing up and hoping things work out. That was really the genesis of it. Then I, being the naive person that I guess I am, thought, *You know what, why don't I try to fix this? I think I have some ideas of how we can connect everybody on a global platform.* Here we are, almost two decades later, and we're still endeavouring to achieve that mission, but I think we're well on our way.'

That's the power of a compelling vision and seeing what other people cannot see.

Your vision serves as the road map. A road map to a higher place, a better future, arenas yet to be explored. There are many commonalities as contributors to success that run deep in the interviews I have with exemplary leaders and industry titans on *Constructing You,* and vision is one of them. How else can something be conceived in the physical reality if it doesn't even have space in the metaphysical realm of your thoughts? Every single building that graces our skylines started with a single, articulated thought. One person had vision and carried it to monumental completion. If you think this sounds easy to do, I challenge you to hold a single thought and focal point at the forefront of your mind daily for 365 days. Only when you have a vision can you truly assess where you are today. How do you know you're exactly where you need to be if there's no future marker to assess it against? Whilst grand and compelling visions are important, they will become perishable quickly if they're not acted on. I know from observation that at this point, majority already rescind and fall off the wagon. You can't talk your visions into fruition, you need to execute them.

EXECUTING A VISION

'Vision without action is a daydream. Action with without vision is a nightmare.' – **Japanese Proverb**

Conceiving a captivating, compelling and magnetic vision is a brilliant start, but it needs to meet reality. This is where advocacy alone doesn't cut it and is a pseudo form of leadership. For example, I could advocate until the end of time for a cause that I believe is worthy, but never really do anything about it – there's no skin in the game, no sacrifice and no real effort. For most, advocacy is repeating what has already been said, putting a few social media posts around it and calling it a day. If you want to see a change, lead by example via *doing*. The transformation is in the execution. It's in the executing of a vision where even more people fall over, for many reasons. First, it looks like work. A serious amount of work is required to get a vision, novel or not, off the ground, whether in a business, local or global industry. That work requires a temporary sacrifice and starting to venture far away from your comfort zone by wandering into the unknown. A leader has to be the person to venture in first, that's why they're the leader. They're the ones who took the risk, who rolled the dice and took a chance, possibly facing ridicule, possibly losing it all. That work requires you to have the belief in your own idea and vision first before someone else does. It requires putting in just about as much of your resources as possible, certainly not only from a fiscal perspective (if required) but certainly time and continued effort. It may require all of the above in an organisation. I can assuredly say that for the past two years (and counting), just about every evening and every weekend has been dedicated to executing my vision, putting it together brick by brick and at all costs.

When Courtemanche was questioned on the building block that has been imperative to getting him to where he is today, it came down to work ethic. 'It's probably mostly built on this work ethic that I bring to work every single day. I don't know where it came from. I have this unstoppable passion to go, go, go. There's a famous quote by Winston Churchill, which is, *Success is defined by somebody who faces failure time and time again with no diminishing enthusiasm.* I'm fortunate I have this enthusiasm. I just keep showing up and running hard and I'm never going to be satisfied till we meet that final objective of connecting everyone in construction on a global platform.'

Further to, is that most people get so consumed with the *how* part of executing a vision at first. Your focus, at first, is on the *what* and the *why*. The *how* will unravel itself when you actually move with conviction towards your vision. 'I'm all about the *what,* so what do I need to do? What is the goal? I'm never about the *how*. I don't care how it's going to happen, I just know that I've set the goal of what it is, I'll let my mentality get me there and drive me there. That's pretty much the key points of success,' says Adra. Usually, the *how* comes dressed as work, and is never what you thought it would look like. Thought Leadership found me as the *how*, but that's not what I started with. I knew what and why. This is why trusting the process is of empirical importance come executing a vision. Did I know with full conviction that not even two years into the journey I'd be writing my second book? That my podcast would reach over 50,000 downloads in a year? That I would have clients in four countries and counting? That I would launch mentoring programs and fill them? Absolutely not. I was promised nothing – not in terms of metrics and not in terms of outcomes. But I remained locked and loaded on the result and the outcome, relinquishing the *how*, yet trusting at all times that the outcome would come. There is no antidote to consistency of concentrated effort.

Then we start hearing an orchestra of excuses. Find me one leader who has had time-tested success, created structural shifts in ways of being and doing that fell into their excuses. Go on, I'll wait. Leaders don't have excuses, nor should they accept excuses from others. You don't get the privilege to lead because you listen to your symphony of excuses instead of doing whatever it takes to deliver your purpose-driven mission. Unfortunately, to most with a mediocre mindset their excuses don't sound like that to them. They sound like perfectly justifiable rationale. The opportunity to lead is a very narrow window of opportunity in your lifetime, however your excuses can be carried with you until death do you part. Adra is no prisoner to excuses: 'It's being consistent in executing and not having excuses on anything in your surroundings, not letting your surroundings be an excuse to not do something consistently and regardless of how hard it is, how painful it is, how easy it is, just stay disciplined and continue. I eliminated excuses out of my life, no matter what excuses I had. That's why I became a solutions guy, because I taught myself that there is nothing we can't solve. There's one thing that should be a barrier in life and it's death. The only thing that can stop you is if you die, and that is it. With that philosophy, it's assisted me in life to get through whatever I'm going through at that time.'

Whilst the reasons for where people fall over in executing a vision are extensive, I've kept it succinct to the insights shared by the contributors, with the fourth being a fear of failure. Can you fathom how many times a leader has failed before you see the success and achievement that they have today? This is, again, earning the right to lead, because you wear the battle scars and bitter pill of experience, as Russo put it, of trying and failing, and getting back out there again and again and again and then once more after you thought you couldn't. The word failure has such a heavy burden and connotation as conventionally understood, but future leaders need to get into a very intimate relationship with failure and welcome it with open arms into their life. When was the last time you, by definition, failed at something? When was the last time you purposely failed so you could learn? I embrace failures, and my list of failures is just about as long as the list of successes. Most people experience one or two failures and quit. That's it, they're spent and they're done, reverting to playing it small and where they deem it to be safe. You will not find a Triple E leader who does that.

Seventeen years in business, Adra reflects that as the rate of failure has increased, success came quicker as well: 'There were a lot of failures that I went through that helped me achieve where I am today. Every time I would do something and it just would not work out, I would not ever look at it in a way that I'm just not good enough, or I can't achieve it. Look, don't get me wrong, there were those few days where I thought, *Maybe I'm not good enough*, I questioned myself, but it would be for maybe two minutes, then, three minutes later, I laughed at myself knowing that I could achieve whatever I wanted.

'Whenever things would go wrong it would just mean that there's more time added now to what I'm working on. I would never look at it as a setback. I'd always look at it as, *I need to give this more time. It's clearly not working. What am I doing wrong?* and I would go into research and research. That's where I said I would work for hours and hours into the night. Just trying to understand how I'm going wrong and how I'm not getting it right until I do achieve. Don't get me wrong, there were times where I would do something wrong for a year. I went and researched, then fixed it overnight. It would take me sometimes a year to fix something that's going wrong within my business, within my mindset, no matter what I was working on. I found that as long as I kept pursuing and staying consistent on my goals, regardless of what I needed to achieve, I stayed persistent on it and did not give up until I succeeded at it. A lot of people don't have that kind of mindset. A lot of people are stuck if they hit a few brick walls – that's it. This is not meant to be, they don't know how to do it, and they're not going to pursue it anymore. I use my goals like a GPS. To give you the best metaphor for this is if you would've set a GPS point somewhere, and you've never been there before, you would need to put it in your phone or your maps or whatever it is to head there but you wouldn't sit down before and plan all the obstacles you're going to face on the way. Red lights, flat tyre, pulled over by police, roadblocks, whatever it is, you don't plan if you're going to stop at ten red lights, and it's going to take an extra seven minutes or so on. A lot of people in life try to plan every step to where they're going to achieve their success. I treat my life like the GPS. I set the address, I get in my car, and I head there. On the way, whatever obstacles come to me, I will deal with them there and then.'

'A leader is one who knows the way, goes the way and shows the way.' – **John C Maxwell**

Nor will you find a Triple E leader shoot from the hip, and proceed without a plan, a direction and distinct consideration in the execution of their vision. I have macro and micro visions, which are broken down into tangible and actionable plans. You wouldn't dare try building a construction project without a plan, letting all the resources run astray and hoping for the best outcome without any coordinated effort. Then the same is applicable as to how you intend to become a leader. What's the plan? Even within the planning you need to have creativity, and conscious awareness of your goals.

Planning is actually the easiest part for Rooney when it comes to leadership: 'I love big picture planning of how we take a big problem, break it down, map out the steps and plan our execution with partners wanting to drive change. It gives me a lot of joy to see the different stages of a project unfold and to look at the progress made together.' Rooney further reflects on how she executes a vision: 'I think the first thing to do when you want to imagine a different future is genuinely sit back and look at the global megatrends, and the change that will be driven from those megatrends. What I would call having an eye on the lighthouse on the hill. Then simultaneously plan the first three things you have to do to walk towards the lighthouse. There's no point outlining a ten-year plan to get to the lighthouse because the pathways move if you're mapping a radically evolving space. But you've got to first find the lighthouse, lock your eye on it and immediately start moving towards it a couple of simple steps at a time. Then replan your next few steps when you're there, because the path to the lighthouse isn't always clear. It's a combination of vision and immediate action.'

SOLVING A PROBLEM

'Leadership is solving problems. The day soldiers stop bringing you their problems is the day you have stopped leading them. They have either lost confidence that you can help or concluded you do not care. Either case is a failure of leadership.' – **Colin Powell**

Solving a problem or exploiting opportunities? However you see it, it's what Triple E leaders are here to do. Whether you are a cadet, foreman, contract administrator, senior project manager or part of the executive team, you can inhabit the function of solving problems for other people. See how leadership has nothing to do with your role, but everything to do with function? Of course, the larger and more complex a problem that you are able to solve for the marketplace will reflect your recognition, progression and consecutively remuneration as a leader. Solving a problem that is recognised by the marketplace, or one that provides a unique solution to the industry, is the foundation of achieving authority positioning. Because in the Thought Leadership world, it's our unique thinking and ability to provide a solution that the marketplace validates and needs that starts bringing people into our world so we can serve them. In continuation of the aforementioned point on advocacy, you need to provide solutions or enable solutions to come into fruition. Simply talking about problems without generating solutions is counterproductive. The construction industry is rife with issues, however, most of the focus is on discussing the issue over and over again. You'll see white papers, events and conferences constantly focused on the issue, not selling the solution. We get it – there's a problem. It's the leaders who focus on the solutions and execute on it. Do you really think high-paid executives, Thought Leaders and entrepreneurs get generously remunerated because they're only talking about the problems? When you solve a problem for people, you're adding value to them. That's what yields reward.

This is why Constructing You comes first – if you're not able to solve problems for yourself, who is going to take solutions from you? You also can't give someone something that you don't yourself possess. Where are your results first? This is why talk and bold words never impress me much, I always look for results.

The Green Building Council of Australia is very much in

the business of solving some of the most pressing problems that have intergenerational consequences if not addressed and resolved today. What is Rooney's framework for approaching problem-solving?

'The first step is obvious: we do our research. We understand the problem. Then we look to partner with others to work out a solution. Then we scope the solution. We sell the solution into markets. Then we implement it, and then we assess the effectiveness of the solution. That helps us work out the next evolution. That's very classic organisational theory. You'll find a whole lot of books that talk about this, but I think the missing ingredient is that people don't often sit in the discomfort of the problem. What do I mean? Sometimes when you have a big problem that you can't resolve, it's really easy to prepare a Gantt chart, compile a table and then put these in a report so you feel comfortable.

'Actually, if it's a big, complex problem, accepting that you don't understand every part of it is the first step. As an example, we're looking to launch a new solution into the residential space because the residential market hasn't actually leaned into sustainability the way we would like. The biggest problem is that we haven't been able to take the volume builders with us – the people that build large-scale in our market.

'We recognised our biggest problem was to find a system that was both rigorous and saleable. Instead of doing the easy thing and rolling out another standard, we spent a lot of time sitting in the discomfort that recognised a large number of these standards – including those we had ourselves created – don't appeal to the decision and change-makers in this market. How do we work with them in ways that are unfamiliar to us to make this change? I could have written a beautiful design thinking process that would have put me back in my comfort zone. Instead, we spent about eight months sitting in the discomfort, working with unfamiliar partners to look at the issue from every angle. It was very uncomfortable at times, but that's the difference between solutions that stick in a complex environment and reports that look fabulous on a shelf.'

What's one of the keys to coming to any solution or result on any scale? It's consistency. Consistency takes an incredible amount of discipline, patience and dedication, and is a reflection of your moral authority as a Triple E leader. This is your reputation that we're also talking about here. If you are someone who changes the plan and course often, your credibility, trustworthiness and dependability as a leader falters. 'It takes a lot more patience than what you think patience is,' says Abraham when reflecting on driving results. And discipline is also at the core of Triple E leadership. Discipline, for a Triple E leader, requires the focused ability to do what they need to do, not always what they want to do, and that may not always be the glamorous work of leadership. If you as a leader are not focused on what's important, you can't expect others to follow suit. Without the disciplined application of effort, where are the results going to come from? A wish and a whim can only get you so far. It's in the consistency teamed with discipline where you will find the quality result that is expected of a leader to deliver. But why aren't people consistent? We can thank the conditioning of people wanting too much too soon, immediate gratification and doing the bare minimum but expecting the absolute maximum in return to start with. This again ties into the need for more patience than you ever thought you needed. I learnt quickly through my entrepreneurial experience to date that the desired results never show up immediately. My mentor always gave me the advice that I was allowed to lick my wounds for an hour, but then I needed to focus on analysing why I didn't get the desired results, put a plan in place to tweak and go for round two (or more). The success certainly comes, but not all at once. However, if you quit after one round, how will you realise the success, or even that moment of clarity where a solution so perfectly presents itself, that you wonder how you didn't see this before. It's what it takes to drive a vision to completion. Your results will always speak louder than anything else as a leader and demonstrating ability to deliver that earns your right to lead.

Consider the following questions for yourself. Sit with them for as long as you need to get clarity on your vision and value:

- What do I really want from my career and life?
- If I could change anything in my life, or the industry, what would that be?
- If money was no object, what would I really spend my time doing?
- What are some problems that I have resolved for myself in the past that others would benefit from knowing how to do?
- Am I willing to stand up for what I believe and the change that I wish to see against all odds?
- When I get to the end of my career and life, what do I want to reflect on and consider it a life well lived?

CHAPTER TWO
YOUR MINDSET

MINDSET

'Anyone can train to be a gladiator. What marks you out is having the mindset of a champion.' – **Manu Bennett**

Take a moment to reflect on the following questions:

- When was the last time I set my mind to something and achieved it?
- Am I conscious of the train of thoughts passing through my mind at each given moment?
- Do I spend more time defending what I already know or do I seek new insights?

- If something doesn't go my way, how long does it take me out for?
- When was the last time I had an original thought?
- Do I know where my thoughts have come from and what's influenced them?
- Am I able to have disciplined thoughts?
- Do I demonstrate surface-level thinking or critical thinking?
- Am I familiar with the different faculties of the mind, and which are the most powerful?

Albert Einstein notably said, 'We cannot solve our problems with the same thinking we used when we created them.' In any model of leadership, it is the quality of your thinking which reflects the results that you have for yourself and the value that you in turn deliver to others. The questions at the start of this chapter were to test your own consciousness of thought. It would seem that in a world of 7.9 billion people, thinking would be commonplace.

'2% of the people think; 3% of the people think they think; and 95% of the people would rather die than think,' markedly said by George Bernard Shaw, Irish playwright, critic, polemicist and political activist. Alas, thinking is not common. The National Science Foundation published an article revealing the average person has between 12,000 and 60,000 thoughts per day. Of those, 80% are negative and 95% are exactly the same repetitive thoughts as the day before. A Triple E leader doesn't adopt this modality of thinking. What creation could come from such mediocre roots? A Triple E leader is one who is able to see the world from a far more critical, discerning lens, can sit with their thoughts and are conscious about creating their own reality rather than being a product of their circumstances. My success as a Thought Leader is a reflection of my ability to sit and reflect on my thoughts and understand how they can be used to solve problems for other people and constantly deliver more value.

As Courtemanche reflected, 'Ideation is one of those mystical things that happens at inopportune times or when you just least expect it.' I truly believe that everyone has a $100 million idea within them, but whether those ideas will see the world or not is a different story. To develop your thoughts, you need to be clear on where your thoughts come from and also what is influencing them. Just as you are discerning about what you feed your body, observe closely what is feeding your mind. Which brings us to the most influential factor of your leadership journey: constructing your mindset.

'Change your thoughts and you change your world.'
– Norman Vincent Peale

We live in a physical world that is a reflection of our inner world, and unfortunately, conventional conditioning has left most people completely disconnected from their inner world, which is also the spiritual world. Over 90% of the results that show up in our world are a reflection of what is happening inside us, not just on the physical plane but the energetic plane. The question is whether you are harnessing the most powerful tools that you have at your disposal, or are you simply relying on one-dimensional, rote, conventional intellect to get you significant results and leaps in your leadership enterprise?

Your mindset is composed of your conscious and subconscious mind, making your mindset the most influential factor in your pursuit to excellence, as it determines how you think, feel, interpret situations and inform the behaviours that you put on display, which of course, informs your results. Mindset isn't feel-good, pseudo-positivity talk, it's simply what will make or break you as a Triple E leader. If you're sceptical as to the relationship between mindset and leadership, you can thank tactical education for that. Leadership development overlooks a specific attribute that is fundamental to how leaders behave, think and learn: their mindsets. Research conducted by *Harvard Business Review* saw that $356 billion is invested annually on leadership development efforts with 75% reporting that they find it ineffective. Learning some tactical skills (which will never work without mindset work first) is the equivalent of putting a bandaid over your problem but never addressing the root cause. Wanting to ascend to Triple E leadership but not attending to your mindset is risky business and fool's play. Adra's been working on his mindset now for ten years to have his paradigms ensure that he achieves what he wants. 'Everything in leadership starts with mindset. Nothing else. Not marketing, not sales, not networking – none of it. It all comes down to what kind of mindset you have, and that will be where your success ends. I consistently understand how to use my mind to achieve what I want to, and that's been pretty much the winner for me, just sticking to understanding how to use my mind to achieve what I need to.'

Mindset isn't as clear-cut as positive and negative, but more a reflection of the beliefs that you harbour. Having a positive mindset is actually reflective of being able to identify and observe the negative, but not be consumed by it. Telling people who have done no work on their mindset to think positive doesn't work; the mind is stuck in the negative with no muscle-power to detach from it into positivity. Either your belief system is supporting you towards your desired destination, or it isn't. Have you recently done a stocktake on the beliefs that you are keeping? When I first started in the industry, the dialogue was rampant as to how many limitations there were in the industry. That progress, remuneration and recognition were all limited, and that the industry is structurally flawed to never allow an individual to realise this. I certainly didn't harbour the belief system then that I do now, so I took this verbatim. Were these beliefs that income was capped serving me? No. Was it the truth? No, because in the world of entrepreneurial thinking there is no limit to how much you can earn, because it's a reflection of value. Except most people haven't developed the thinking to deliver the value for sustained periods of time to get the income that they desire – there's a difference. My career changed when I shut off the limiting beliefs that infiltrated the broad dialogues in the industry and worked on influencing what I could. The only ceilings that exist in the industry are those that you've built for yourself when you stopped working on yourself. It's not the industry's fault, not your employer's fault, not the team, not the project, not the management team and not the leadership team. You chose to internalise limitations that weren't set by you, instead of working on you to make yourself so brilliant, so good and so exponential in your abilities that the only ceiling you have is the time on this planet.

And if you reject this idea, then you're speaking from the same limitations that you haven't chosen, only to justify not moving forward and growing. My results of recent speak for themselves. I changed my belief to, *I can develop the skillset to influence my own income*, instead of, *No-one in the industry is going to pay me what I desire*, and the former belief became conducive to supporting my goals. A previous limiting belief was, *The only way to be an industry leader is to work my way up the corporate ladder*, whereas I changed it to, *I see myself as an industry leader today and I am more than capable of causing scale change*. Adra shares the sentiment: 'It's having belief and it's setting a goal and actually knowing you can achieve it. I've had people tell me what I'm trying to do is impossible. *You're never going to get there, you're not so-and-so, you can't do it. You don't have a billion dollars backing you, you can't do it*. Fortunately enough, I've proved a lot of people wrong in that journey.'

Your belief system will determine how you even see failures. Failure is only fatal if you call it your finale – that is, you call it quits too soon. Most people experience one or two minor failures and call it quits for the rest of their career. Adra has experienced failure many times over, but his belief system doesn't recognise that as even being a failure, it's still a success: 'When I do something and I fail, the world calls it *failed at it*. Maybe I didn't make money from it, but without a doubt, I will carry so many lessons from it that whatever I go and pursue after it, or if I repeat it and start from scratch, I'm going to do it ten times better. I gained a lot of success from whatever some people will call a failure. That's why I don't believe in failure. My only yardstick is success. No matter what I do I have succeeded in. Whether I open a business and it doesn't work out for many reasons, and then I've moved on from that to a different venture, it's still success to me, because I'm winning and I learned something and I moved on to implement what I learned in something even better and greater, and it just means that I made a decision that that thing was not to be for me.' Imagine if you adopted the belief that failure isn't fatal or final, and that there was no such thing even. You would be a far more convicted and confident person, which will reflect in your leadership standing and value. There will certainly be times when the conviction and confidence will be tested, but harbouring beliefs that are wholly conducive to success will always place you in brilliant standing in the long-term. Adra was touted as the kid from school who would either end up dead or in jail, having dropped out in year eleven, but he had one belief supporting him: *I will achieve.* The rest of his results speak for themselves.

As much as I would love to go down the esoteric rabbit hole and explore the depths of our conscious and subconscious powerhouse, the attributes of a mindset of a Triple E leader have been extracted with concision from the contributors. This is the baseline to start the journey of truly knowing the power of your mind, and maybe it's even bringing it to your consciousness for the first time right now. For if you cannot control the discourse and disposition that is first happening internally, you won't be able to sustainably achieve whatever it is you choose to pursue, let alone connect and change what's happening in someone else's mind. Most people can't change their own minds, so they'll never be able to change someone else's. As the great Russian writer, Leo Tolstoy said, 'Everyone thinks of changing the world, but no-one thinks of changing himself.'

EXTREME OWNERSHIP

'Extreme ownership. Leaders must own everything in their world. There is no-one else to blame.' – **Jocko Willink**

Extreme ownership is a universal concept, popularised by Jocko Willink and Leif Babin in the namesake book. Remember the first line of this book – it all starts and ends with leadership – therefore, it all starts and ends with you. A Triple E leader has deeply internalised the notion that all the results that show up in their life, their work, their business, are a direct consequence of their internal and external workings. Leaders do not look for scapegoats, externalities or other people to pass on the responsibility when it comes to performance and results that they are responsible for, both for themselves and any situation where they've assumed leadership capacity. A leader must take full onus – positive or negative. Think about the word responsibility. It's a composite of response and ability. When you adopt the framework of extreme ownership it allows you to have the ability to respond. This is extremely empowering, both on a personal and professional level. I know very well that if a result I desire hasn't shown up in my life, it comes back to me, and I have full ability to change that. Yet it is when people look to pass blame and not realise that the buck stops with them that standards start slipping, which is no model behaviour of a Triple E leader.

Before the defences come up, there are extenuating circumstances that are extremely out of a leader's control. Whilst the event – like economic disruption – is out of the realms of control, the response isn't. Defeatist attitudes have never really gotten anyone far. If you're working on a project and your team is under-performing, missing milestones and risking deadlines, that's on you because there are levers that you can influence to change the trajectory of a project. Respect for a leader automatically drops when they'd rather wipe their hands clean of a complex situation. Respect compounds tremendously when a Triple E leader knows that it's fundamentally their responsibility. If your client isn't fulfilled with your services, that's on you to meet client objectives. If you gave a subordinate a task and they didn't fulfil it, that's on you, as you could have explained it or demonstrated it better.

'I've got staff that have been with me for seven, eight, nine years and regardless of what mistake they make, I find myself to blame,' says Adra. 'Always the way I approach any mistake or simple thing that's gone wrong, I approach it in a way of, *Where have I gone wrong? Where haven't I explained or taught you or given you the right resources to achieve it properly?* Even if I have ten times before, there's still something I'm doing wrong with that person under my control, as they're not achieving what they need to. I don't make excuses. I don't find that if people are making mistakes that are in my organisation, it's their fault. It's my fault, it comes back to me. Maybe I'm not providing the right training; maybe I'm not supporting them or giving them the right resources. It starts with you and ends with you regardless of what way you want to think about it. It's unfortunate in this world, nobody actually sees that. I have this conversation with so many people and a lot of them disagree with me, they believe that your surrounding has a big impact on you, which I actually don't believe at all.' Very rarely are people willing to shoulder the blame and put their hand up for responsibility when things go wrong, but of course will be the first to do so when accolades and recognition are being doled out.

A Triple E leader will constantly reflect and evaluate their experiences to identify what they could have done better and differently to achieve the most victorious outcomes – for themselves, and for others. As much as this concept is applicable to all pillars of leadership in this book, it has to come under you first, as if you cannot take full responsibility for yourself, you cannot do so for others. Experience only has value if it's evaluated and the lesson extracted. Otherwise, the experience is just rinsed and repeated with no further value. Most professionals rest their laurels on their experience, but if it were to really be evaluated, it's just one year of experience repeated twenty times. Where's the growth in that? If someone is lax and complacent in one arena of their life, that's going to be reflected in other arenas. How you do one thing, is how you do everything. This is also why experience alone is never the marker that makes a leader. Someone may go through experiences but never extract the lesson. Why it was a good or bad experience matters more than the experience itself. Then it doesn't matter how many years of experience or value of projects delivered if they keep on repeating the same mistakes over and over again. This in a cornerstone of progress and developing wisdom and insight.

> 'The moment you accept total responsibility for everything in your life is the day you claim the power to change anything in your life.'
> **– Hal Elrod**

Extreme ownership is intimately intertwined with leadership because the qualifying factor is that once it is taken, the leader is driven to do something about it. Otherwise, the same mistakes and outcomes will show up again and again. What do you think will happen to your leadership status and credibility when people immediately around you start noticing that you're taking yourself and other outcomes that you have going on into your own hands? People will start to respect you more, trust you more and believe in you more. You will also find some Triple E leaders take onus and even have the drive to solve problems that they didn't cause. Yet, they have a deep sense of ownership over it, and treat it as their own. Rarely will you hear a Triple E leader say 'that's not my problem' or engage in any form of self-pity that they have to deal with problems they didn't cause. The first step into this mindset is to stop blaming any sort of misfortune that you are experiencing on anyone other than yourself. Your excuses can be with you until the end of time, but the language of leadership has no space for excuses. If you listen closely to the discourse and dialogue that Triple E executives, founders, leaders and entrepreneurs have, they don't lay on the excuses. In the same merit, if you're not able to take extreme ownership for yourself and control your own outcomes, then there is no demonstrated ability to do that for others at a level that surpasses mediocrity. This does, of course, require discerning thinking to ascertain what is in your locus of control and what isn't. If you can't control it, let it go. So tell me, who's in charge around here?

EMOTIONAL VOLATILITY

'If your emotional abilities aren't in hand, if you don't have self-awareness, if you are not able to manage your distressing emotions, if you can't have empathy and have effective relationships, then no matter how smart you are, you are not going to get very far.' **– Daniel Goleman**

On a past project that I worked on, certain project managers displayed extreme emotional volatility. Construction sites have a tendency to bring out the emotional side of many, due to the pressures and risks associated with project delivery. In high-pressure situations, said managers would slam chairs, yell, stomp around, slam doors shut, be holed up in their offices, engage in heated phone conversations (yelling matches). Was this a kindergarten or a construction site? I wasn't too sure sometimes.

'If you come in and you shout and you rage, then everyone else is stressed. If you work through challenges in a realistic but manageable way, then there's a pathway for everyone else to do the same thing and it helps you lift your people up,' points out Rooney. This isn't to say that a leader needs to be clinical. You can still have a lot of care and consideration for what you do, but losing it every time something goes wrong isn't necessary. You may feel better in the moment, but have you thought about the negative energy you're passing onto others? What message does such volatility send to subordinates? They'll have extreme hesitation to approach you, as the response could be anything. In times of extreme pressure and uncertainty, a subordinate will not follow a leader who doesn't have predictability or consistency in how they react. It doesn't instil confidence by any measure. You have to be able to control your emotional state and disposition in leadership functions. If you cannot control your own reactions, you really cannot be responsible for leading others. My favourite analogy which perfectly summarises controlling your emotional disposition is to be a bottle of water. When a bottle of water is shaken and has pressured applied, it will not go everywhere when opened. However, when a bottle of soda gets shaken and has pressure applied, it's going to explode. It's very easy to be reactive in certain situations and let the emotions cloud judgement, clarity and direction, but that's not what gets people with leadership aspirations to the top.

The key leadership attribute of reducing the amount of emotional volatility is emotional fortitude. Why do so many people quit in the pursuit of leadership? It's tough. When you are a leader, you're the one who starts standing out and having larger aspirations than most. Society can sometimes be akin to being in a bucket full of crabs – when you try to leave, they'll work very hard to bring you back down, especially if you start generating a social presence for yourself. The vitriol that gets thrown my way because of my person and what I stand for has already come, but I was ready for it. You know you're doing something right when not everyone agrees with you, and I'm fortunate that many certainly don't agree with me. Especially when people's belief systems are challenged – or when they see someone doing something that they really want to do and attaining more success than them – the attacks come. Just look into history to see that anyone who has stood up for a cause, to deliver a message or to illicit change has been met with some form of resistance, attack and vitriol. But I can take it – and I have to, as sitting in silence isn't the alternative. I could've packed it all up ages ago had I listened to the negativity that was thrown my way. But only people who are achieving less than you will criticise you. A key leadership attribute to be Triple E leader is therefore resilience and fortitude. I love the word fortitude, as it reminds me of having a physical fort around you to protect you from incoming assaults. It's the resilience to be able to outlast those who didn't have the emotional fortitude to keep going, because they were more concerned with what others thought than being the disruption and leading with high standards. Anytime something new is introduced to any industry, it will be met with hate. Do you think everyone in the industry welcomed Miram's introduction of a five-day work week? 'I choose to take [the criticism] as a compliment, we've got them rattled and that's a good thing. It's a compliment, we're doing the right thing.' The benefits are clearly articulated, and it wasn't change for changes' sake, but the vitriol that came her way was not only professional but personal. That wasn't a deterrent to continuing to revolutionise how the industry runs. You have to be able to bear the stones, as much as the accolades and awards.

Kurzydlo reflects on the important attribute of resilience to leadership: '… Resilience is a key to staying on that path even if it does change – resilience to know you've done the right thing or resilience to know that you need to get back up again after you have been knocked off. People wouldn't believe the amount of times that others get knocked off – the amount of times I've been knocked off. You have to pull yourself back up, and get up that next day and believe in what it is you are trying to achieve. You eventually get there and when you look back, you reflect and say, *I'm glad I actually did that. I'm glad I found the strength to get back upon my feet. I wasn't feeling great, but I did it, and look where I am now!*

That incredible feeling of success and fulfilment does not come unless you have that determination and built resilience as a person. But you need to remember that resilience grows. You grow and you get more resilient as every challenge comes your way. It's only in hindsight and reflection that you look back and can see how resilient you have become from the unexpected challenges you have gone through. Everyone goes through moments in their life and career where they didn't think they'd be able to push through, but they have. Every time you push through you become more resilient – you grow and you learn and you're then onto the next challenge, which is even a bigger challenge than the one before, but you can handle it because you're more resilient!'

Triple E leaders wear a certain type of armour. Think of a king. A king wears his regal robes, but under the robes, he has his armour. A little stone doesn't find its way to our heart so easily, because we are so mission driven that it's simply not feasible to sit around and exert energy and focus on what other people think, because more often than not, they have proven that they don't. Imagine the hardship and turbulence absorbed by those who have headed global movements and humanitarian changes, like Malcolm X, Mandela or presidents during wartimes. When my going gets tough, I listen to *Can't Hurt Me* by David Goggins (and journal). He came from no privilege or comfort but from the depths of family abuse and has turned himself into an indestructible human being. Physically, mentally and spiritually. Those who troll, or come out to criticise leaders, don't know the depth of inner work we do before entering the arena. It's not so easy to knock us down. But we are all human, and words do hurt. The key is to work to reduce the amount of time that they get you down. I certainly haven't brought it down to one hour to get over it, and I'm certainly not one to forget so easily either. Those who have never stood up for anything, let alone themselves, will never fathom the backbone and courage it takes to be different and speak out, in a society which is equivalent to crabs in a bucket, ready to pull someone down and back when they seek an alternative route. This is being the tip of the spear, and the strength and resolve of a person who chooses to be the tip of the spear should never be underestimated.

Your spiritual, physical and mental houses need to constantly be in pristine order to be a Triple E leader. Yet we have people who explode over the most minor inconveniences, exerting unnecessary energy and stressed out by the same. Being tempered is important; you need to know what deserves a reaction and what doesn't. But those who can apply that discretion will see them advance. Look at the senior personnel around you – are they able to stay focused under stress? Are they able to maintain a balanced outlook in complex, difficult environments? If two people were both going for an executive promotion, and one had the proven ability to remain balanced, focused and in control of their person in high-intensity situations, who would be more likely to be given the chance to lead? Nonetheless, we all have our buttons and there are times when an emotional reaction is the only way we can respond. It's important to know your triggers, and if you fall down nine times, get up ten times.

This certainly isn't a call to suppress emotions, for the leaders with a strong heart – not just head – are those with the most devout followers. How rare it is to find leaders not just with a strong mind but a good heart too? It's about emotional regulation, and understanding that you need to learn to manage, process and respond to your own emotional state first before you can resume leadership positions at large. We are human, and having a disconnect from our emotional side will also blind us from seeing what others are experiencing in certain situations. You know, before we develop our brain in the womb, we develop a heart. We first had a heartbeat as a sign of life. Remember, though, that overdone negative – or even positive – emotional reactivity is a choice. The skill is observing the emotion, but not becoming or being consumed by the emotion.

CONTINUOUS LEARNING

'Most experts and great leaders agree that leaders are made, not born, and that they are made through their own drive for learning and self-improvement.' – **Carol S Dweck**

Your education shouldn't cease at the end of a degree – quite frankly, that's where it should begin. You've just learnt what everyone else has learnt, now what? The professional marketplace is relying on the rote and antiquated learning completed years ago to still have merit and relevancy, and afford them any sort of real progression, recognition or remuneration. If your learning stops, in any arena of your life, then you have lost the right to lead. The rent is due daily when it comes to leadership, and you have to be evolving and growing at a faster rate than anyone else. How else will you be able to see more than what others can see? This hunger for learning comes from a natural curiosity and also commitment to the vision, because the more that I know and am able to provide distinction and unique perspective on, the more I can serve and benefit those around me. But learning has to be directed, concentrated and focused, not sporadic and loose. We don't have time to learn everything about everything, let alone implement it to achieve mastery. Courtemanche learned early on that what makes him tick is practical application of knowledge, and learning when it's applicable to what he's trying to achieve. Diatribes and sequential reading for regurgitation didn't resonate, but that didn't mean that the learning stopped. As a Triple E leader, you constantly need to engage in purposeful learning and refine your subject matter expertise. This isn't to say that leaders need to know it all, but they certainly need to make concentrated efforts to find out. And this requires taking your own development into your own hands. If you follow my content, you'll know that the greatest project you'll ever get to work on is you. And agreeably, you can never be active enough when it comes to developing yourself. It's unfair, when you think about it, that one lifetime isn't enough to learn, implement and master all that we need to lead a fulfilled and aligned life. Your learning needs to be selective and relevant to where you are right now. There's a whole host of areas and topics that I would love to know more about right now, but I know that it won't provide me with the greatest quantum leaps in my development. There is no antidote to the sweat equity, friction and investment of time, energy and finances to grow. The only way to bypass the time is to get a mentor. The time that most people spend looking for a way around it could have already been more effectively utilised.

The motive behind continuous learning is also impressed in the fact that leaders should never be satisfied. If Triple E leaders were satisfied with the status quo, well, that doesn't actually make them leaders because they're not driven to impart any change or disruption to the industry. If you are satisfied with the current state of affairs, then your curiosity to develop new ways of working, doing and being is quelled. 'It is what it is,' is a saying that has killed more opportunities, dreams and innovations than we can fathom. But if you know that things could simply be done better around here (which they can, for the avoidance of doubt), then you will have an insatiable desire to learn. It's a costly mistake to make to stop learning. Mirams holds the same conviction: 'Just have a thirst for learning and knowledge. We always want to be improving, so just be open to ideas, be hungry to learn, read as much as you can and challenge your thinking.'

But if you're not learning, then you've stayed married to your comfort zone, and it's universally accepted that nothing good comes from your comfort zone. Thinking you're a leader yet being married to your comfort zone is a sign of mediocrity and nothing that a Triple E leader would ever subscribe to. If you're not putting yourself in situations where you're being challenged, trialled and tested, where is the growth going to come from? If you don't have the appetite to risk anything, or have any skin in the game yourself, then don't think you'll just inspire people through your words. All that I have learned in the last two years alone, to just get me here, is about ten years condensed into two. However, I know that there is still a significant amount that I don't even know that I don't know, but I am driven and determined to learn it so that I can constantly stretch myself and reach for things that are extremely out of my comfort zone. Did you think that your sheer hard work at just doing your job would get you Triple E leadership status? The consequence of not continuously learning through your own accord is that your relevancy in the industry will expire. It doesn't take much to become a dinosaur in the industry. Everything in the industry from policies, materials, methodologies, legalities, laws and regulations to people and performance is constantly changing. 'That's what keeps me motivated to continue learning and taking on new challenges,' remarks Russo. 'As a leader within Johnstaff, that leadership role has grown. As that's grown, I've certainly looked at getting more training. I've done some formal training. We've done informal training within Johnstaff. As that leader and manager, you also need to make sure you remain current in the work that your team is delivering.' If you are not constantly feeding your mind with new ideas relevant to your own development to work on yourself, and remaining ahead and relevant in the industry, then it's time to make it a significant priority.

'Champions do not become champions when they win the event, but in the hours, weeks, months and years they spend preparing for it. The victorious performance itself is merely the demonstration of their championship character.'
– Alan Armstrong

Growth is commonly misconstrued as being organic. That if enough time will pass, time will lend itself to growth. Assuredly, that's far from being the case. To me, that's why 'years of experience' in industry carries little weight, for it could be one year of experience repeated twenty times. So, time doesn't equate to growth. Your long-term success as a leader is going to be dependent on your hunger to learn, as the facets and skills that make up Triple E leadership are mostly nuanced and intangible. Remember, leadership in itself is not a skill. It's a function supported by a particular skill set. American author and leadership coach, John Maxwell, devised a leadership growth process which I want to share with you here to demonstrate the structured and deliberate nature of learning required to achieve inspirational heights. Consider this framework as you now take a conscious approach to learning rather than a loose, organic approach:

Phase One – What you don't know you don't know – this is the stage of learning where you may have the most blind spots, and where ego and ignorance teamed with lax and complacency stop most people from entering the arena of growth. Not too dissimilar to most people reading this book, I also came up through extremely conventional pathways and started my career in construction, and these pathways never divulged a fragment of the chasm of knowledge, insight and wisdom that I have self-generated and garnered. It's a fool's game to think you already know what you need to know. If that was really the case, would you only be where you are? In this stage, it's about accepting that you're at the start of your growth journey and it's time to run into the discomfort.

Phase Two – I know that I need to know – this is the stage where you bring yourself to the starting line of daily immersive learning of leadership principles, strategies and skills. Notice that skills come last, because until you don't understand the principles, you also don't know what skills you need. It takes humility at this stage and a fierce commitment to learning. I know that in this lifetime alone, I would have never learnt a fragment of what I have was it not for being mentored by Ron. I stood at the outset of the Thought Leadership pathway knowing with all my being that I needed to know this, it wasn't even an option to not go on it.

Phase Three – I know what I don't know – this is the stage of having consolidated the specific things you need to learn, and having become very deliberate about your learning. The success of this stage is determined by you generating and implementing a plan for intentional growth. No brilliantly delivered construction project happens without a plan, so how can your learning possibly go without one? This stage also requires you to defer gratification and sacrifice resources – time and/or fiscal. The day you start learning is not the day you emerge as a Triple E leader. Akin to a construction project, the resources required from preliminaries to trades are well articulated at the outset of a project, and the same applies for you. Do you need a mentoring program, new experiences and challenges, books and podcasts to flood your mind with daily? Take stock of the word *deliberate*. If you want to create an impact, then a focused approach on branding, messaging and communication is required, not another degree.

Phase Four – I know and grow and it starts to show – if you have done stages one to three, well, then you are allowing the effects of compounding to come into play. Imagine where you can be after ten years of daily learning? Your efficacy as a Triple E leader is demonstrated over the long-term, and the progression, recognition and remuneration start to come. During this period, more and more people are coming to you for insight and knowledge.

Phase Five – I simply go because of what I know – Triple E leadership is now your natural disposition, it's your permanent state of being and doing. You are able to navigate the complexities of leadership with finesse, and your ability to lead is one that is spoken about, hopefully with a mix of awe, inspiration and reverence. You've completely levelled up, and now it's time to go again.

Before you move on to the next chapter, take a moment to honestly assess where you are, without ego or judgement and home in to your commitment to your leadership development. Those whose names live on past the test of time have always gone all-in on their mission. You never hear of anyone who was lukewarm about their mission, now do you?

CHAPTER THREE

YOUR PERSON

WHO YOU ARE

'To find yourself, think for yourself.' – **Socrates**

When I first entered the industry, I assumed the notion that leadership looked a certain way, informed by the majority of people that I saw in leadership positions. Based on the narrow thinking I had at the time, it seemed that to achieve the same positioning, I would need to follow suit. So, I did. Like waves eroding the cliff shore, being anything other than myself was hugely detrimental and erosive to my being. The erosion happens slowly but surely, until you get to a point in time when you can't even answer the question, *Who are you?* I lost my sense of self completely; lost in the sea of sameness and not being able to articulate the internal friction and conflict within. I thought my power would increase by fitting in, when the real power was to step into my own light and prerogative of standing out. I went from a place of being meek, dulled down and diminished, to bold, expressive and confident. I was on track to becoming just another face in the crowd. The construction industry has a dominant and suffocating ability to draw the perception that being in construction looks, sounds, walks and behaves a certain way, which results in a sea of sameness. If you doubt this, go to your site or workplace tomorrow and see how many people are in full expression of themselves (and not all dressed the same). The experience in the industry at the outset wasn't dissimilar for Rooney: 'I feel really fortunate that the term authentic leadership was coined in the last decade, following positive psychology research and business studies, because in my early years, I didn't always see myself as a leader … In some of my earlier corporate roles, I almost had to pretend to be tougher than I was – or than I wanted to be. Leaders seemed to carry a big stick.'

A dangerous trap to fall into is to try and emulate leadership styles of predecessors because it's worked for them. But that's the thing – it worked for *them*. I tried emulating what I thought leadership in construction looked like, and the only thing it did was backfire and burn me. You don't need to learn the same lesson the hard way. 'If you aren't authentic, then you will struggle to lead effectively and sustainably,' says Kurzydlo. 'If you struggle to lead and empower others, you'll struggle to grow a business from a financial position, let alone a people position.' When you are thinking of the type of leader you are, close the doors to the outside world and first look inwards.

It was only through the discovery of the Thought Leadership model of entrepreneurship and leadership that afforded me the realisation of my detrimental mistake; that leadership *is* about being all of who you are. And leadership certainly doesn't have one framework or perception in which one must fit into in order to lead. But the issue, as I had experienced, is that most people can't be all of who they are because they don't know who they are. How much time have you actually spent figuring out your person – to the absolute macro and micro of what you are uniquely positioned and here to do? If you can't tell me your mission, vision, passion, purpose and core values in less than a minute, you don't know your person well enough. A person who is consistently all of who they are is Kurzydlo. She reflects, 'Authenticity definitely is connected to knowing who you are. Once you do know who you are, it actually isn't that hard to really walk your walk and talk your talk. You back yourself, you believe in yourself, you know what you stand for, you know what that means. And if people don't like you, that doesn't bother you because you were there to be who you are and influence.'

It's the same for Nathan, who has a direct approach and can cut to the heart of a situation fast, but this wasn't the leadership disposition he led with when he first started out. In a world full of copies, or unforgettable people, the greatest gift you can share is your authentic self.

It is a disservice to the people around you to not be in full expression of yourself. Because I had followed convention, I was left feeling dull, diminished, meek and dissatisfied. That's no position to lead from. Was it not for the mentoring journey I went on to first understand myself first before anyone else, in order to magnetically and congruently lead with that, I wouldn't even have the honour of writing this book for you. Leadership starts with you, because people, first and foremost, connect with people. But you cannot put yourself out there if you don't know who you really are. Who do you think will follow you if you are a chameleon? You'd be better off being a leopard – they don't change their spots. But why don't people step into their full power and presence?

'It's not important to be liked and a lot of leaders talk about this. It is important to have influence on people – a positive influence. If everybody tries to be liked by everybody, then you're definitely not being authentic because it doesn't happen that way, not everyone likes everybody and that's just the world we live in. If you are true to yourself, and you act in a way that is what you stand for, then you are being authentic and naturally people will gravitate to you, regardless of whether they initially like you or not.' As Kurzdylo correctly states, it's not to be liked. It's not to appease the masses. Most people place far too much weight on what other people think of them that they lose their sense of self in the process. I know, I used to do just that. You cannot, as a leader, be something for everyone. You should rather be everything for someone.

Think about these questions to commence clarity on your person:

— What are my top seven unyielding values?
— What was I uniquely put on this earth to do?
— What will make my time on earth worthwhile?
— What am I naturally brilliant at?

- When I do _____, I lose all sense of time and it drives my energy up.
- What qualities do I most admire about myself?
- If I wasn't afraid, what would I love to do?
- What am I truly passionate about?
- What makes me feel alive?

Your value system as a Triple E leader is of empirical importance, as it will display to others what is and isn't acceptable to you. It will also allow people who share parts or most of your value set to come into your world and want to be led by you. Kurzydlo confirms, 'It's quite important that people know their values and sit in those values no matter what situation they find themselves in. That is authenticity. They aren't pushed and pulled to align themselves with certain positions, if they don't feel like that doesn't align with who they are. It very important that you diplomatically stand up for what you believe in.'

Rooney also lives in congruence with her value system, but this is where many falter: 'There's knowing your values and then there's acting on them. That sounds easy, but it's relatively complex. Positive psychology has a lot to say about living your values. But actually being able to define and name your values – that's hard. But it's also hard to say that you are values-led if you can't define them and then you can't use them in decision-making processes.' I certainly share the sentiment.

At an event in 2018, an exercise was given to name our top four values. I pulled out my phone and drew blanks. This was a stark moment for me – how could I be driven but not know what I value? Today, having done the internal work to determine so, I make decisions with ease because I know what I value in my heart of hearts. The thing with values is, you don't choose them. Society can be all too quick to want to rearrange your values for you and change the sequence of them, but that will only leave an individual living out of alignment both inside and outside of the workplace. But once you identify your values, the only way to live in congruence with them is blanket application, not partial application. For example, some may say, 'I believe in diversity and inclusion of thinking ... [but not in this instance],' or, 'I believe in equity in the workplace ... [but not in this instance],' or, 'I believe everyone should be fairly paid ... [but only under my conditions].' Selecting where and when to apply your values doesn't make you virtuous, it makes you a walking contradiction. Resolving this alone in your leadership journey will start clearing up the fog as to who your authentic self is. Only then can you function in accordance with that.

Now note that people will first buy into the individual and who they are before they can be sold a vision. To communicate your person in a controlled manner is where your personal brand comes into play.

PERSONAL BRAND

'A brand is the promise of an experience.' – **Alexander Isley**

When you have clarity over your person, that gets captured, expressed and articulated in a personal brand. A personal brand is not a series of colours, logos and templates that you like from Canva. The construction of a personal brand is a strategic, detailed and an extremely thought-out process that happens from the inside out – not the outside in. It took me just about one year to inhabit and develop the personal brand you see today, making it one of the most distinct in the industry. Without a personal brand that is an extension of your person, there is a lack of congruency in how you portray yourself. In the Thought Leadership world, our brand is the most important asset, as it allows us to communicate and connect our person, message and philosophy to our target audience. An authentic and magnetic personal brand is also what will announce what you do and don't stand for and voice your message, allowing your impact and influence to have far broader reach. When this is expressed, your influence grows, because people aren't knowing you passively. I know without a doubt that the opportunities, collaborations and clients that have come my way in a very short amount of time are due to my brand. I do find that the type of people who work in construction like things to be concrete – pun intended. This amount of input yields this output. Except a brand is an intangible asset that is constantly evolving and has infinite potential. Because most cannot see the possibilities from the outset, they refrain from constructing their brands altogether.

However, it's not that professionals don't have a personal brand – they do. It's just one that has had unconscious effort put behind it, or very surface-level thinking, which ensures that the individual gets misunderstood and not heard and seen for who they are. A brand is not an accumulation of projects you have worked for, as someone cared to advise me (incorrectly so).

Having a personal brand for a leader is imperative, as it's what offers the distinction between you and others. Your brand conveys your identity, uniqueness and distinctiveness. Your brand clearly articulates what people can expect from you. The professional world is mostly sleeping on the opportunities that come with having a brand. When a company first goes into business, it's a brand that is generated. People are not exempt from this. When I first started on the journey of The Construction Coach, I haphazardly, with superficial thinking, put together a brand that was based on externalities and an unclear message and value proposition that had nothing to do with me – everything that could have been was out of alignment, and Elinor Moshe, as a brand, was nowhere to be seen. I cringe when I come across collateral from the early days, but it also serves as a great reminder of how far it has developed. My business and my personal brand weren't talking to each other, and I was continuously misunderstood. Fast forward to today, there is no mistaking who I am or what I stand for. This brings people who want to be part of my world into it and repels those who cannot stand me. I wouldn't have it any other way. My brand speaks *for me* before I have to, but I am hyper-conscious of constantly managing the brand and experience that comes with it. But before a brand is built, you need to understand who you are, what you stand for, what you believe in, what you're here to uniquely do and why, and the promise of your experience. You may be thinking, *Well, there are leaders in the marketplace who are leaders, but haven't developed a brand.* You're correct in your observation, but having a brand enables you to bypass the time it takes to get to the top because you're standing out in a credible and notable fashion with a high level of distinction. I know, because it's my brand that has afforded me exactly that.

If your brand is the experience and the asset that broadcasts what you do and who you are, it all needs to be in complete congruence with every part of you. You see, irony is fascinating. There are people wanting to be mentors and coaches, but not doing the one thing themselves they want mentees to do – invest in themselves. There are people preaching lessons about entrepreneurship, yet never risking anything like one. There are people who pre-qualify themselves as leaders, but don't even have a single vision for *their* life, let alone someone else. Being a walking contradiction will only get people so far. There is a stark contrast between what people preach and what they do themselves. Always look behind the facade, for there's typically not much holding it up. And to be a leader, your existence needs to be in congruence. You do what you say, you say what you do. You don't simply talk the talk and do absolutely no walking. You post inspirational quotes, but have done nothing inspiring. You talk about taking risks, but when it comes down to it, you'll never roll the dice on yourself. You talk about integrity in your values, yet that's only extended to people who suit your belief system. Your followers and the people that you're looking to serve will be able to see right through the holes in whether you live in accordance with your brand or not. Remember that people fundamentally follow people, but for them to decide if that person will be you, means it's time to invest in constructing your personal brand.

NATURAL DISPOSITION

'If you spend your life trying to be good at everything, you will never be great at anything. While our society encourages us to be well-rounded, this approach inadvertently breeds mediocrity. Perhaps the greatest misconception of all is that of the well-rounded leader.' – **Tom Rath**

The power of knowing who you are is to then lead with your natural disposition. My prerogative is to stand out and be front facing. I didn't choose that, it's what I was given. I don't thrive in environments or with work that is highly technical or detail orientated, and I also really don't like management roles and functions. I'm the visionary and the dominant front-facing force, the one who sets the grand vision, the direction, and brings the rocket fuel to get there. So, when I am in that arena, doing just that, I'm in alignment with my natural strengths. I used to work in ultra-technical environments, and I didn't understand why I was so depleted and would have no mental capacity for anything. It's because it wasn't in line with my natural grain. At the same time, ideation and creation is also a natural strength of mine. I have an abundance of ideas for my business and how to add value to the industry, and certainly apply my own discipline to see them through, one by one. Communication and public speaking are also my natural strengths, which makes podcasting, content generation, writing books or speaking in any forum an absolute divine time for me. If I had to demonstrate and live out my leadership doing tasks and working on projects that weren't in line with my natural disposition, my leadership (and career) would be dulled down and I would be suffocated, plus, nothing would ever really materialise. I don't try and do everything in my business either, and I consciously seek out others who are the best at what they do to compliment me.

In consideration that a key function of a leader is executing a vision, knowing yourself is also closely intertwined with this. Courtemanche has previously commented that when someone is faced with an idea, they're first to go examine themselves, understand how they tick and tap into that source of inspiration. Why is this critical?

'Well, it is probably the most foundational, critical piece of any career,' says Courtemanche. 'It's not easy to do because everyone's ego wants to make us believe that we can do just about anything. We need to take that moment and actually reflect on where our passion comes from, because passion is the thing that's going to propel you out of bed … You can't fake that passion. I'm not good at finance and I'm not great at marketing, and if I had to focus on those things, I would still be struggling to launch Procore today. It's not easy to do, but I really do encourage people that want to see their passions all the way through to some form of success to really look at that. My uncle, Jack Courtemanche, worked in Ronald Reagan's White House in the United States back in the 1980s. He was Nancy Reagan's Chief of Staff. I asked him the question, *How in the world did Ronald Reagan become president?* He was an actor. My uncle said, *He knew his weaknesses and he staffed the people around him to support him that would allow him to be successful.* I never left that behind, and I always did that.

I found Steve Zahm, who has been with me since the dawn of Procore. He went to business school, and his strengths, plus my passion around product and engineering was able to propel us to where we are today. It is about learning your weaknesses and really homing in on your strengths.' If you don't know your person well enough, then you also won't surround yourself with the people who will compliment you. I wholly agree with the quote at the start of this chapter that a leader doesn't need to be brilliant at everything. But to be brilliant, we need to stay in our zone of genius and let others shine in their areas of genius. My value is better placed writing a book, rather than editing a podcast, but I know that because I know myself very well as I've taken the time to learn myself – which is never-ending as we are expansive, ever-changing and limitless.

The power of your leadership is going to be best experienced when you stay in your lane of strengths and have the captivating vision to band others around you who have bought into your vision and want to make it happen. Remember:

You don't have to be the loudest

You don't have to be the most colourful.

You don't have to be the smartest, either.

You do have to be *you,* and that's the strength which will allow you to emerge from the shadows with silent power.

SELF-IMAGE

'It's hard to lead a cavalry charge if you think you look funny on a horse.' – **Adlai E Stevenson**

Before I could show up in situations as a leader, I had to see myself as one. Being a leader has been impressed and recorded into my self-image, which informs everything that I do. I absolutely love the quote at the start of this section, because so many people think they look ridiculous being a leader yet want to position themselves as such. And they think they are ridiculous when they have to post a photo on social media or get up and present – it seems foreign and silly if it doesn't align with your self-image. Your self-image is the subconscious framework of how we see ourselves and our lives, notably coined by Maxwell Maltz, an American cosmetic surgeon and author of *Psycho-Cybernetics*. To shape how you see yourself is to first exert influence on yourself, and again you need to do that before you can influence others. The issue is that most people generate their identity and self-image from externalities, such as their job title, the company they work for, projects they've delivered, past events, cultural and societal conditioning and so on. If you aren't aware of the filter through which you see yourself, then this will impact how others see you. Again, if you were hoping for a tactical take on leadership, this is far from. Changing your self-image to align with your vision and the entire person you wish to be can be extremely challenging, but it would be negligible of me to omit one of the most influential factors on your success.

'Our self-image, strongly held, essentially determines what we become.' – **Maxwell Maltz**

Most people carry a very high level of self-consciousness when it comes to putting themselves in the limelight, or at the front of the pack. Have you noticed how people start shrinking, adding doubt to their sentences, receding away from the limelight when they start feeling self-conscious about themselves? These seemingly small actions have very loud consequences for a leader. Your followers and subordinates notice absolutely everything, leaving you under constant watch and observation. Even the slightest unconscious concession made by you will be reverberated widely. As Adra explains, 'Fix your mindset and work on your self-development. That's probably the best advice I could give anybody. Before you even consider writing a business plan, write what kind of person you are and how you're going to deal with other people.' Without a redefined self-image, leaders end up dealing with imposter syndrome. When a leader has an immense lack of confidence in their ability to lead, it shows itself to the people around them. Have I had doubt along my journey? Certainly, but it was fleeting and didn't dominate my actions or behaviours. When people say seeing is believing, it first starts with seeing in your mind's eye before anywhere else. Think of every building that lines our skyline – it first started as an image in one person's mind, didn't it?

Your self-image is key, but leadership still needs to be earned. The rent is due daily when it comes to holding your leadership authority. Kurzydlo continues, 'Just because you are a leader doesn't mean that you have the right or the authority to instruct people.

You need to earn the right to lead. You need to earn that trust and respect, and once you do, you can communicate effectively because they will listen. It's when leaders don't earn that trust and respect from their people that their leadership won't work, it doesn't matter what structure you have in place, it won't empower.' See yourself as the global leader – the greatest organisational leader the business has seen – but never let that override or neglect the results and performance that are expected from you. However, once you start seeing yourself as the person who achieves a certain level of the aforementioned, you may find you approach situations with more clarity, conviction and confidence, which informs your results, and so you're setting in motion a very powerful force and upwards momentum. This is also one of the influential factors that determine whether or not someone gives up. If you don't see yourself as the person holding authority, then when that gets challenged, when the problems start coming in – you'll quit. But you won't be diminished or deferred so easily if your self-image is aligned with your vision and goals.

This section, along with the other principles listed, work to cumulatively provide you with one key thing: confidence. It's not that you don't have confidence right now; it's that you've chosen to repeat the narrative to yourself that you don't have any. As such, this reflects in your aura, disposition and right through to your actions. Confidence is sexy, and because most have such a perceivable lack of it, they gravitate towards those who exude it. Confidence is a characteristic that followers do look for in leadership. To have truly lasting and unshakeable confidence first comes from recognising all of who you are and how divine and limitless in spirit you are. It comes from the implementation of all that I have been discussing insofar. I constantly get asked, how do I have so much confidence? Well, here is your answer. There is no chance I would have the following I do was it not for being in full expression of my person and giving myself permission to be confident. To some, it's confidence, to some, it's arrogance, to others, it's intimidation. None of their perceptions are my business and neither should it be yours. You unlock the confidence within you, and watch your leadership expand and transform.

SUPPORT SYSTEM

'The one who follows the crowd will usually get no further than the crowd. The one who walks alone is likely to find themselves in places no-one has ever been before.' – **Albert Einstein**

Leadership is lonely. For a very long time the sentiment of 'it's lonely at the top' didn't mean anything to me until it became my reality. I am fortunate that I am someone who highly enjoys solitude and values my own company. And the viability of my leadership is heavily based on the quality of my thinking, creativity and innovation, which for me is best fostered alone. Growing up an only child has always allowed me to be great by myself. I've been training for leadership my whole life. But as you seek to pursue a purpose-driven mission, the challenges come, and they are greater and can cut deeper than anything a corporate career can throw at you. Some may choose to wear their independence as armour, wanting to valiantly brave the leadership journey alone. But to be the beacon of strength, light and inspiration to your community, you too need an incredibly strong support system around you. Personally, I've had to learn how to ask for assistance and not front that I can go through the trials and tribulations by myself. If there's a support system the industry can be thankful for, it's this one. Did you know that Mirams had initially said no to the opportunity to be the founding CEO of Roberts Co?

'Initially, I said no. I didn't think I had the pulling power to get people to leave their steady, secure employment. Most of them were the breadwinners to come and work with me on a wing and a prayer that we'd build a new construction company so I said, *No.* Three months later [they] came back to me and said, *I want one more crack at you and then I'll leave you alone if you say no this time.* I still couldn't decide what to do. [They] rang me one day and said, *What's your advisor saying?* who's my husband. I said, *I don't know. You talk to him,* and so [they] did. Paul, my husband, and George know each other well, and they went and had a coffee and my husband came home and he said to me, *You've got rocks in your head if you don't do this, but it's entirely your decision.* How different the industry may have been was it not for the support network and people who can see your potential.

'What first happens when you start evolving and growing, is you disconnect with many people. This is a natural consequence of growth, because you are evolving but they have selectively stayed in the same place. I have disconnected from just about 95% of people that I used to know, only a mere two years ago. And I am glad that happened, because it allowed for space in my life for people who had more to do with my future than my past, aligned to who I was becoming rather than who people once knew me for. But I know that I wouldn't have been able to work through the low lows and the high highs of the leadership journey were it not for my core support network. You only need five people in the world to believe that you can, and that's all you need to carry yourself forward through testing times. Was it not for the unwavering, dedicated and unyielding support of my core inner circle, I would have slowed down on my path, reconsidered my pursuits and played smaller than I should have.'

You don't need a lot of people, you only really need to surround yourself with a handful of quality people, and you will go further and faster than you thought possible. This support system has been the key building block to getting Kurzydlo to where she is today: 'The support is incredible; but there are certainly moments where you don't always feel that support, and I know that there's a lot of leaders that feel alone at times and feel that no-one believes in them. Or that there's doubt in yourself. But reflecting on why I believe leaders are ultimately successful is they've had that unwavering support from people that believed in them and that are always there to help them believe in themselves. For me, it comes back to a family of love and support and having that real resilient group around you. You somewhat create this for yourself too, because you give back to them in a similar way – you create the network around you that is supportive. It's a two-way street.'

A natural part of authority, which contributes to it being lonely at the top, is creating a certain distance between the leader and the follower – but it naturally comes with the territory. Colin Powell, former US Secretary of State put it as 'leaders are above but never beyond'. The distance is also required in order to exert and hold the authority, and there is a common misconception that leaders need to be approachable. The qualification is that they don't need to be approachable *all the time*. Of course, if you are a leader that no-one wants to tell anything to, your source of information that informs how you lead is severely impacted. People will not be moved or led by those they perceive to be just like them. It's inevitable that those in charge get treated differently, and rightfully so. They've earned the right to lead, so that comes with a certain level of respect and reverence. It can also be a stark difference to a leader from being 'one of' to the 'only one', which at first brings a certain feeling of disconnect. But this is necessary, as what you are now concerning yourself with is not what the masses are concerned with. This experience wasn't different for Mirams: 'I had a lot of friends that I suddenly couldn't be really friendly with because I was suddenly their boss. Before I became a director, I was reporting to them and with one promotion, they were now reporting to me. Luckily, I worked with great people who coped really well with it, but that's hard to do. You're now the boss, you can't share everything you're thinking every day, every minute with your staff, and there are things you need to filter and that only you know. Leadership can be very lonely.'

But feeling lonely is different from actually being alone. Whilst you may have the strong support of close friends and family, the ultimate support in my experience has been that of my mentor, Ron Malhotra. A mentor is the ability to stand on the shoulders of giants. Kurzydlo experienced the same benefits of having a leadership mentor, as someone who early on in her journey challenged her, pushed and pulled her as to what it meant to be a leader, and allowed her to emerge in the strength and resilience of the person she is today. Mentoring is the unique opportunity to bypass the time required to learn the insights, lean into the wisdom and experience of those who are already where you wish to be. If you wish for people to invest in you, then you first have to invest in yourself. As leadership authority John C Maxwell said, 'One of the greatest values of mentors is the ability to see ahead what others cannot see and to help them navigate a course to their destination.' The challenges and failures that you are more than likely going to encounter in your leadership journey have more than likely been experienced. You can lose time, burn yourself continuously, and never realise what you don't know you don't know if you don't engage a mentor. The right mentor can be your key to sustained success. Plus, leadership is complex because you are dealing with the greatest variable of them all: people. In all the diligence and determination that I have to succeed, I wouldn't have been able to synthesise, implement and garner the principles, mental models, frameworks, and then the skills that Ron Malhotra has taught me. Leaders don't have the ego to think that all they know right now is all they need to know to lead. It's a fools' game to be playing if you think that to be the case and is certainly no attribute of a Triple E leader. Where most people falter is that they will seek to engage a mentor or a coach once they 'make it'. Do athletes engage coaches once they've made it, or when they were starting from zero?

And finally, your support system is required because to be on a continuous leadership journey requires sacrifice – or as I prefer to name it, deferred gratification. Behind what people see, which is the sexy side of leadership, is a lot of friction that goes into growth. A leader is the person who has sacrificed more than those they are following, and will continue to do so because leadership is earned, not granted. I have invested more into my own development than most people do into their entire careers over a lifetime, including fiscally, emotionally, mentally, spiritually and time wise – and it's only just begun. I have deferred gratification on what other people deem to be 'fun' or things that I 'should' be doing at my age. Not that I consider whiling my time away to external stimulus 'fun'.

Adra shares the same sentiment, recollecting how every dollar he made was reinvested in him and the business, and 'giving up' a lot of the conventional youth things. But fun was working on the business, and now he is thirty-three years old he has total time freedom and choice. This deeply resonates with me, as I have done – and am doing – what most won't even contemplate, and sometimes in the thick of it, the mind can temporarily question it all. But that's when the support system kicks in. And the higher up that you go, the cost increases. So be prepared to invest, with all the equity you have, to be a Triple E leader.

When asking Slattery about the key principles pertaining to leadership, she brought up the topic of luck. 'People talk about getting lucky and we often say at work, *Oh, wow, we are so lucky.* You need to be capable and competent, leverage every opportunity, and then you "get lucky". I think it's a great leadership lesson – working hard to get lucky, instead of waiting for it to happen. In this way, we can have an element of control over how lucky we are. I do believe I'm lucky, but I also think you've got to put yourself in the right place and get out of your comfort zone to get there. It comes with an enormous amount of effort and focus.'

I encourage you to consider the following as you now need to look at strategically building your inner circle. And don't feel bad for setting boundaries, not everyone needs to have access to you. The people in my inner circle have learnt that they either bring the fuel, or they need to get off the ride. Consider the following as you go do a stocktake of the people closest to you:

- Are the people in my inner circle growing at the same pace I am?
- Do they have a positive influence within people in their own life?
- Are they high-energy people who discuss potential, visions and ideas?
- Do they hold themselves and others to excellent standards and reject mediocrity in every aspect of their lives?
- Do I want their results? (If you don't want someone's results, you also don't need their advice.)

Construct wisely, for your inner circle can make or break your success as a Triple E leader.

PART TWO
CONSTRUCTING OTHERS

Not everyone loves to see others thrive. Some want to see you do well, but not better than them. Some may work so hard to impress their world view on a follower, completely disregarding their vision and ambition. And some will simply have no care and consideration for the success of their followers altogether. The aforementioned makes up a high percentage of people in the industry, surprisingly so. Yet there is the small percentage that is more concerned with enabling the success of those around them. For their success makes up their own success. Constructing Others starts to move the perspective from you alone and onto improving those around you, in whatever way, shape and form is tied to your vision. It's in this transition phase that you'll start to learn that leadership is less and less about the individual, but more about the mission and enabling others to achieve what they want. Not what you want for them, but what they want. There's a huge difference. However, just because you know what's right and good, doesn't automatically mean that people will go along with you. This is where we start to look at developing high income and impact skill set to nurture and lead your follower base.

You see, to lead is a duty not to be taken lightly, for it's the highest honour and privilege a stranger bestows on you. Many want the accolades and recognition that comes with leadership, but not the deep sense of responsibility when it comes to delivering on it. People who were once strangers now significantly rely on me. They've chosen my guidance, advice and direction to ensure they achieve what they want. When my clients get off a call with me, when they have chosen to turn to me, the expectations are very high, and rightfully so. It's not just someone's career that you're dealing with, it's their life, it's their person. It's per above, the experience someone has in your team or organisation. To have the honour of being the leader means you're the guide and who your followers look to. Triple E leadership sees droves of people who you're surrounded by become their best, and this is leadership of the highest standards, not for the faint of heart, and not for those who only use their mind and not their heart.

I don't think you can ever capture every single minute nuance that comes with dealing with and leading people, as human beings are so fundamentally complex, transient and temperamental. For the first part of your career, your technical skills will be required, but past those early stages, your technical skills won't save you. Understanding how to lead people towards outcomes will. The principles and insights contained in this section of the book can also be applied to leadership at large, but for all intents and purposes, the findings contained in this section will enable you to bring people along with you, so you can get the best out of them. The only qualification that I will put around this is that if an individual or subordinate has no inner interest in going where you wish to go and what you wish to achieve, then no tool in your toolkit will move them. Understand that most people on a low frequency and energetic state only have consideration for themselves and their best interests. If they don't see value in your vision, don't waste your time and effort convincing someone who simply doesn't want to be there. When you also go on the journey of Constructing You, you will come out on the other end distinctly *you*, and accept that you cannot and should not be something for everyone. You won't be everyone's favourite – that's impossible.

CHAPTER FOUR

THEIR POTENTIAL

EXTRACTING THEIR POTENTIAL

Let's look at a construction project. Labour commonly makes up the largest component of an estimate, and what takes the most man-hours to schedule, plan for, coordinate and manage at every single stage of the project. Therefore, to achieve excellent project outcomes, what do you have to do? You need to get the absolute best out of the individuals first – not the most – the best. Sometimes the most is the best, but it's still the best. It's amazing then how most people who aspire to get into leadership, let alone Triple E leadership, then spend most of their time concerned with the technical skills and not about knowing what is required to make the biggest difference to projects. It's constructing others and getting the best out of them. That's your function as a Triple E leader, and where those who work with you end up will be a testament to your ability to achieve that. This certainly isn't to suggest that people around you are broken, and that they need to be fixed in order to perform. It also isn't here to suggest that people don't inherently have within them what it takes to be brilliant – they do, but their mindset, conditioning and own limitations don't allow them to see that. One of the most valuable functions I carry out as a leader – and a mentor, of course – is to hold up a mirror for people to see clearly in. Constructing Others is looking past who they have been and look to who they can be, then enabling them to get there. But if you haven't expanded yourself, per part one, then you aren't well-served or deserve to construct others. Remember, a leader can only take you as far as they can see. And if the furthest they can see is next week, well, therein lies your answer.

Constructing Others is also about giving space and permission for those around you to also construct themselves. I've come across faux mentors and leaders in the industry who tried very hard to impress their world view and way of being onto me – it had nothing to do with me. It was a total disregard of the person. In the same merit, very few environments, especially in the corporate space, foster a place to be all of who you are at work. There's more fulfilment when you can be 70% of who you are, versus 20%, if not 100%. Only those who don't know who they are bring this pseudo-professional demeanour devoid of personality to the workplace. Like I said, I don't expect you to agree with all that's included in this book. Being a Triple E leader is about, 'Helping them find permission for the skills and attributes they already have in other parts of their life, to let them know they're welcome at work,' says Rooney. On further reflection, Rooney says, 'It's giving people permission to have a presence in the workplace and justification as to why that presence is important. Sometimes, you're not teaching new skills. You're giving people permission to use skills that they already have. This is an aspect of authentic leadership; you need to bring the whole person to work. It's all about being yourself and supporting others on their own journey ...' When you create the space for people to bring their whole person, not just the CV version of themselves, you are edging them closer towards their potential instead of telling them to leave it at home.

Extracting the potential of your followership is closely tied with showing them what's possible. Possibility is what ignites people, a dream can instil renewed hope and fuel. Dr Martin Luther King Jr did have a dream after all. I remember in the early days of my mentoring journey with Ron where he was expanding my own realm of possibilities. Even if I didn't believe it then like I do now, I believed the belief that Ron had in me, and set out with a plan of action against the milestones I had to meet. And I delivered on them. And I got more and more excited as to what else I could do and create. Not once in my eight-year corporate career had someone sat me down to look at all my naturally aligned possibilities. If I had waited on that to happen, I again wouldn't be writing this book. Quite the opposite actually – the conversations were based around trying to fit me into boxes. Out of all the questions I hated being asked was, 'What do you want to be though?' and the only response that they would understand was a job title. How limiting is that? What do most people have in store for you? Nothing. Now imagine a Triple E leader that can fill the hearts and minds of the followership with all they can be. Away from convention and societal conventions, away from linear trajectories and suffocating boxes. There's the realm of potential. Most people judge others based on their past experiences, which can be measured rather than their potential, which is infinite. However, when you can't see limitless possibilities for yourself, you can't inspire and ignite that within others. Infinite possibilities are tied to the fact that we are extensions of the creator. Call it the creator, divine intelligence or what you will, we are not just physical, sentient beings. I have no doubt some will scoff at this, considering it to be 'woo-woo'. We have access to imagine anything that we desire, and then make it happen. There is no limitation to imagination and creation, and that's where infinite possibilities come from. Until you truly develop a deep inner standing of this, you're keeping a lid on yourself and those around you.

However, you can't just *tell* someone that they're infinite and anything they set their mind to is possible. In a heavily left-brain dominant society, you'll just be disregarded. Not just with this, but with any idea. This is where the skills, rather than lofty ideas, start to come into play. When most attempt to pursue leadership ambitions, they start with the tactical skill set. How do you know what skills you need until you know what mindset you have? That's why mindset development always comes first. I realised that the traditional skill set I developed through conventional education wouldn't allow me to carry out my vision. However, I could only identify the skills I needed once I knew what the vision entailed. It perplexes me why those who aspire to leadership go do another generic certificate. I haven't heard of any Triple E leader who's collected certificates and degrees and achieved world-class impact and influence. Have you? The first universal attribute that Triple E leaders need to possess to get the best out of others is influence.

INFLUENCE

'The higher you want to climb, the more you need leadership.
The greater the impact you want to make, the greater your
influence needs to be.' – **John C Maxwell**

People on a low-energy vibration and frequency cannot influence anything around them. This is why constructing you comes first, and there is no leadership without it. If your own passion, purpose, vision, mission and living in alignment with your own values don't excite and electrify you and awaken you to the human experience, then I am not sure what will. For it is exactly that which will ignite the fire within and start to raise your frequency to become an energetic match for your vision. This is when people who want to be part of your followership will start banding around you. I share this not as to sound esoteric, but to serve you and highlight the most influential and important dimension when it comes to impact and influence – energy. Sure, you may be able to implement a tactic and influence the people in your office, maybe your immediate family, but that's not all you're here to do, is it? The higher the energetic plane you are on, the more people that you will be able to influence. Just look at the greatest religious leaders in history, they were enlightened beings. If you disregard the energetic state of your being when it comes to influence, don't be surprised when none of the outcomes you desire show up in your life. Have you ever really been inspired and ignited when you were around someone who was as energetically flat as a pancake?

The terms leadership and influence are not interchangeable and are also not one and the same. Influence by definition is having 'the capacity to have an effect on the character, development or behaviour of someone or something' and to cause something to be changed. One can be influenced for good or evil. Influence is a tool, or a strategy, that a leader will deploy when required.

Russo reflects, 'It means being able to give people options, but ultimately, for them to be able to come to a decision themselves. It's not forcing a particular direction upon someone else.' Influence must also not be confused with authority. Tenure and status don't carry much weight in the face of inspiring action and maintaining momentum. Neither does obedience inspire.

'I think the leaders who don't have influence maybe do default to authority and then they will struggle to grow as a leader,' says Kurzydlo. Most people will have an adverse reaction come the term influence, but it's not a bad thing, as what matters is what the source of influence is. We are all influenced by a variety of sources, except most don't apply a level of discretion to their sources. And right now, you already possess a level of influence. The difference is that leaders have heightened awareness of their influence and work to control and extend it. When you have a compelling vision that a select followership wants to be part of, you are in a greater position to use influence for good.

'Leaders are also exceptional readers of a situation, and that's what exemplifies their influence. Harvard and Yale research psychologist Priya Nalkur-Pai disserts, 'They are self- and situationally-aware. This means they understand how their focus, behaviours and beliefs influence others, but they can also read the situation to understand what kind of language, behaviours and beliefs are needed.' This means being sensitive not just to what is being said, but what isn't being said. Triple E leaders don't go into conversations, meetings or the like with any pre-conceived notions about the other person, as that limits their ability to influence the followership in a new direction, but also limiting how their own beliefs and biases influence a situation. Whilst this may sound simple, few people are sensitive to the nuances of human psychology and behaviour around them. The real skill of leadership and business is the ability to get people to take a specific and desired course of action that is mutually beneficial. But to do that, you need to have a true and deep inner-standing of the other person. I am sure that most conflicts and differences could quickly be de-escalated and resolved if people spent the time understanding the other person without bias and predetermined notions. For an industry that is truly about the people and less about the projects, why people do what they do is pivotal. Don't you wonder why the most influential part of our existence – which is understanding self and others – is excluded from conventional education? When it comes to influence, you both need to see the broader picture of an individual – which is appreciating their culture, motivators and belief system, but it's not about harbouring biases which places a cap on them. It requires you to look at a situation for its merit yet understand the contextual influences at play. That's situational awareness.

'If you can't influence people, then they will not follow you. And if people won't follow, you are not a leader. That's the law of influence.' – **John C Maxwell**

A key part of being able to read a situation is to have a heightened appreciation as to what drives your followers. Whilst there are nuances between each individual, there is a collective driver between certain types of people based on their origin, upbringing, culture and the like. Triple E leaders know the intricate scope of intrinsic and extrinsic motivators that drive their people. Appreciation and praise needs to be given in a way that suits the individual, as recognition is important. If you don't know what's important to them, you won't be important to them. 'You have to go through the genuine process of understanding what's important to them. You have to be prepared to walk a mile in their shoes if you want change that will be embraced by everyone,' says Rooney. I once worked on a project where I would explicitly express what was important to me to get fulfilment from a role, only to be met with confusion as to how it could possibly be that I simply didn't fall in line with everyone else or enjoy doing what everyone else was. The subpar management that I was subjected to failed to see an individual, only a resource. People are far more nuanced and complicated than that, and assuming that everyone takes the same satisfaction and fulfilment from the same work as others is a stifling mentality. Your duty as a Triple E leader is to learn how to truly extract what it is that people want, but to a greater extent, know what they need. Because you can't assume that most people know what's good for them. If you need evidence on that, you don't need to look further than people's health, finances, career prospects and spiritual connection to see that most don't do what's good for them. When you have extracted this pivotal information, then you have strategically positioned yourself to influence an outcome for an individual or a collective.

But why have influence? Why is the discourse between leadership and influence so intricately intertwined? It's so you can express influence *on the outcome*. Do you simply have a track record of results or not? You will find that most people cannot influence outcomes for themselves in their immediate circle, as they're not even aware of what they can influence. Are you influencing everything you can in your career and life at the moment? Where most people start to rescind and dull their influence is when they consider all too much what others may say and prefer to be liked rather than get things done. 'It's about your influence on the outcome, not about whether people like you or not. People will grow to support what it is you stand for, what it is you are driving naturally, from your strong business influence and your consistency. If you are consistent in who you are, what you do and your message, whether they like you as a person or not, they will support you. That is something I've learnt over time – it is not about likability. Leaders do not have to be liked in order to be respected,' reflects Kurzydlo. 'Influence is about your effectiveness, and if you can't project influence, the people around you won't be sparked into action, and you will certainly not be able to fuel momentum,' Kurzydlo continues. 'You may have initial action, but momentum behind that will not continue. Your influence is critical to inspire action that is appropriate to the business because if you don't have that influence, you will continually be battling and struggling with your communication for what the business is trying to achieve, which won't result in profitability, growth or diversity and what you're trying to achieve in that business. I think influence is absolutely critical as a leader.'

Note that influence cannot simply be built by facts and figures, which is playing to an individual's intelligent mind. People aren't rational beings, despite how fervently some claim themselves to be. Influence comes from refining the skills to bypass the intellectual mind and connect with the emotional mind. Emotions are what captivate and enthral us – why else do people sit through two hours of movies? – it's not for their logic or intellect at times. That's why knowing the driver set of your people is imperative, so you can connect to it and have ability to apply positive influence in your leadership value.

COMMUNICATION

'You can have brilliant ideas, but if you can't get them across, your ideas won't get you anywhere.' – **Lee Iacocca**

When was the last time you learnt how to speak? Just because you know how to use language, good grammar and articulation doesn't mean you know how to connect, sell or leave an impact with the whole of your speaking. If you listen only to speak, you will miss valuable insights and wisdom that are being passed onto you. You see, just because you learnt to speak and listen when you were three, doesn't make you exemplary at either one today. To speak is common play, but to think distinctively, connect, transform and captivate is an art form. A study done by the Economist Intelligence Unit found that ill communication contributed to added stress, failure or delay to complete a project, low morale, missed performance goals, presented obstacles to innovation, slowed career progression and even lost clients. From experience, so many errors on projects could have been avoided with communication that was clear and concise, and also transparent when it needed to be. As a leader, you do need to repeat messages again and again. Expecting people to hear something once and have their behaviour adjusted doesn't work unless you are one of the greatest orators who can inspire the masses. Research by the *Harvard Business Review* concluded that when communication was repeated, it was more likely that a project would be completed faster and with fewer mistakes. If you haven't already, make sure that you also listen to the full interview with each of the contributors of this book and take note of how they communicate.

Contrary to popular belief, I used to be a poor communicator. Average at best. The degradation started when I stopped being in full expression of myself because it was intimidating to others (certainly not my problem today). So I would mumble, losing confidence as I went, placing way too much emphasis on what the other person was thinking as I was speaking. That's also a key detriment in communication – placing all too much emphasis on yourself, rather than the audience. The corporate world then continues to stifle expressiveness, with most speaking in this pseudo-professional monotony that, quite frankly, doesn't make it clear if someone is even present in their own conversation because of how bored they sound. This wasn't the voice of a leader; this wasn't the speaking that someone who desired impact and influence had. I spent most of the last decade trying to amalgamate my speaking to suit the requirements of others, and that led to a complete erosion of this very important skill. There was even a time where I couldn't stand to listen to the sound of my own voice – assuredly, I don't have that issue anymore. But think about the most inspiring talks you have heard, the speeches that have moved you the most. What has resonated with you, stayed with you and moved you? I still get people connecting with me online because they heard me a year ago, or people recollecting a specific lecture or webinar I did from months ago. That's just a snapshot of what happens when you construct yourself to be a Triple E orator, because you won't reach great heights without exceptional communication skills. The art of communication is one that simply takes time to develop. The first time I picked up the microphone wasn't the time when I recorded my best episode. The first content video I shot was certainly not my best take. The first panel event and speaking engagement were not the best. It took time to develop my messaging and articulation, both written and verbal, but it was a deliberate course of action, and that's what is necessary for Triple E leaders. Having a conscious focus on developing the most important skill that supports your leadership function cannot be underrated. There is no leadership without world-class communication ability.

'There's many times I've seen communication happen, but the digesting of the communication wasn't what the deliverer intended it to be. Clarity of the communication is key for a business leader to ensure that the vision and the mission is understood clearly.' – **Melanie Kurzydlo**

The key part of excellent communication is to illicit action via delivering a concise, clear and convicted message. That's the only way your communication ability can be measured. To do this, first comes the work on Constructing You. Where conventional communication training falters is that it focuses on the tactical only. I could give someone a winning slide deck and a script to pitch, but that doesn't mean that they will still know how to use the tool for maximum impact. The conviction in your messaging comes from being truly connected to yourself, your self-image and your vision. When I tapped into that, my voice changed to have this natural authority, projection, fluidity and depth to it. Your voice is an extremely powerful vehicle, and when you really think about it, it's what connects your inner world to the outside world. Poor orators over explain, have an immense amount of filler words and simply place words in sentences and call that communication. If your followership isn't moving in your direction, then your communication isn't facilitating them to be their best. You will also find that over time there won't be a followership.

'Courage is what it takes to stand up and speak,
courage is also what it takes to sit down and listen.'
– Winston Churchill

Typically overlooked when it comes to communication is listening. It's not just what you project outwards, but what you are able to retrieve inwards. Listening is not just listening to what is being said, but to what isn't, and it certainly isn't listening to respond. If you are only in conversation with people who can reaffirm what you already know, you're never going to stretch and grow. If you get defensive when you are challenged, protecting your existing beliefs and ideologies, you're leaving behind opportunities to see what's possible (and also not listening). This isn't just about active listening; this is listening with an open mind, a blank canvas of no preconceived thought, and being in, and only in, that one conversation. In a world of hyper-connectivity and a myriad of distractions, being hyper-attentive is invaluable to someone's experience of you.

It's not intellect that rules conversations, it's emotions, as was touched on previously. People are not rational beings, they're complex. Naturally there are those who are heavily analytical and rely on their intellect to see the world, but even they need to deal with emotions, in themselves or in others. The communication technique of emotional intelligence is the 'ability to understand, interpret and respond to the emotions of others', according to *Psychology Today*. Emotional intelligence is about being able to separate your vested interest in a conversation and guide the dialogue in your mind, and to pay intense attention to what is being said. But to also get to the root of the issue, which can sometimes be hidden under a cloud of emotions (especially onsite, which is a heated environment at times), is the ability to ask fantastic questions. If you're not asking yourself difficult questions and sitting with your thoughts and responses, how can you guide someone else through such a conversation? So many questions daily are superficial and surface level, and as a Triple E leader, your line of questioning in any situation needs to be distinct, refined and able to get to the root cause of an issue. When you do this, you're able to lead others from a deep place within them and truly move them, because you have facilitated a connection above all and can see the person and situation for what they truly are.

Your communication strength and ability are going to be tested the most during those tougher conversations. As a mentor, I'm the first to support, applaud and promote my mentees, but simply only communicating the good things they're doing doesn't equate to the transformation or the results that they want. The first time that I had to have a hard conversation with a mentee on their performance and involvement was confronting, but there was a way to do it and it had to be done. That's one of my duties as a mentor, to hold up the mirror to my mentees to show them their blind spots and set them back on course. You can reflect on your appetite of choosing the hard and sometimes uncomfortable conversations in other arenas of your life – do you front them, or sweep them under the rug and hope for the best? But if not for the Triple E leader having those hard conversations, you're not proving to be a service to those around you. You're actually keeping them at the same level, but with everyone else moving around them and they're actually regressing.

'Having those hard conversations may be difficult, but you are giving them a gift at the end of the day, by providing them feedback on where they need to improve or where they need to look to grow, where they need to educate themselves …' comments Kurzydlo, as well as reflecting that owning and having the hard conversations whilst still supporting the outcomes is a key function of a Triple E leader. The hard conversations usually show the harsh truth of success and few people want to hear it. They'd rather hear the sugary or watered-down version. It's actually in the avoidance of having the tough conversations that a worse outcome is generated. 'A lot of people struggle to have those hard conversations because they believe it's going to end up in a worse result. Whereas, more often than not, if they're thought through and planned prior, the result and the outcome will actually benefit even more than the original intention because that person then respects and admires that you've brought that hard conversation to the table. Generally, if not in the first or second meeting, that hard conversation will result in a good relationship outcome, but also a good business outcome,' says Kurzydlo. Is there a tough outstanding conversation you need to have?

DECISION-MAKING

'In any moment of decision, the best thing you can do is the right thing, the next best thing is the wrong thing, and the worst thing you can do is nothing.' – **Theodore Roosevelt**

Subordinates and followers turn to leaders who *make* decisions. In times of crises and ambiguity, clarity is fervently sought. In reflection over the past year alone, each time there was a sign of how we work changing, people onsite immediately turned to the leaders to see if they miraculously had any further direction. Uncertainty tends to suffocate, which is often mistaken for people being averse to change. The not knowing can cause people to leave an organisation in search of security, which I have seen time and time again during my corporate experience. It's the same when clients turn to me when they're in a conflicting situation – they seek clarity and a decision (I never make a decision for a client, but mentor them on how to do so themselves). Considering the high-pressure, complex environments with competing demands and varying amounts of information at any given time, construction offers a unique framework in which decisions need to be made, also at varying speeds. Having a refined ability to make decisions is a key attribute of Triple E leadership, and this too is one that can only be developed through action. Successful people generally make decisions fast and change them slowly, whereas unsuccessful people make decisions slowly (sometimes excruciatingly slowly) and change them quickly. A fast decision doesn't mean shooting from the hip, but once all the critical factors which may affect the result of the decision and all other known considerations have been analysed, a decision needs to be made. Of course, context does matter. We don't want to see fast $100 million deals and slow breakfast decisions made. When questioned on executive decision-making, Russo reflects, 'It's the people and personal elements that really play on your mind and you run scenarios over and over, but at the end of the day, you can't ignore those tough decisions, and the tough decisions are what ultimately define you as a leader. They're the things that are probably most visible to the team that you are leading. Once you've made the decision, you need to be able to back it up and stand by it.' It's one thing to navigate the waters when they're calm, but your definition of character will come to play when you can make the same quality decisions through tougher times.

But how do executives, leaders and entrepreneurs mostly make decisions? Once skills, knowledge, experience and sometimes seeking consensus has been exhausted, it all needs to be connected at a level of higher intelligence and then reverted to your intuition. A 2016 KPMG study at the C-suite level found that only one-third of the 2,200 CEOs surveyed trusted their data and resulting analytics, and according to the PwC Global Data and Analytics Survey, 59% of decision-makers say the analysis they require relies primarily on human judgment rather than data. Your intuition is your internal guidance system. Kurzydlo reflects on the power of the 'gut feel': 'I listened to my gut and went with my heart and that has served me well throughout my life. In using that gut instinct to make decisions about what's going to be right for you, and not necessarily listening to other things out there in the ether, has been the best decision I have made in my career.' Kurzydlo continues, 'I think it's ensuring you do have the right information to make those decisions and make those calls. If you make the wrong call, as well, it's owning it, then rectifying it and what you're going to do going forward, so in the future, other people, if they're in that position, will understand what to do as well. Also, it gains credibility. You gain credibility by not always having the right answer, but by rectifying or standing up and owning what it is that you as a business leader need to do in that position.'

It's not intellect alone that will give you the conviction and confidence to make a decision. Over the last two years I have made many decisions that were not based on rationale or consensus, I just felt that they were exactly what I needed to do. The thing with intuition is that the more it's followed, the greater the confidence you have in it when it's telling you if a decision is right or wrong. But above all, that's only something that can be assessed in retrospect. Slattery reflects on the value of trusting your instinct and backing yourself: 'As a leader, sometimes you've got to trust the feeling in your gut. If there is a niggling feeling, a certain reluctance, it's important to consider why. It doesn't mean pulling the pin, but more than once I've made it further down the track and wished I had trusted myself more. In the same way, if your intuition is telling you to go for something, back yourself all the way. Of course, sometimes you'll look back in hindsight and feel you've made the wrong decision, but it's about recognising you did the best you could with the insight and information you had at the time.'

Why do you think the leaders at the C-suite or of an entrepreneurial streak are remunerated like they are? Because they're the ones who take the risk and responsibility when it comes to making really difficult decisions. How many difficult decisions have you made to date? How did it feel when making those long-term projections? Let's look at it from a personal perspective first. Most people cannot make a few thousand-dollar decisions for themselves in terms of investing in a mentoring program. The same people aren't just going to have the decision-making muscle developed to make six-figure decisions for themselves, which may be seed funding for a business idea. You cannot go from zero to hero and make great big decisions without making many small yet calculated decisions with risk along the way. Now in the professional context – if you're not making great project decisions worth thousands of dollars, why do you think you'll be entrusted to make million-dollar organisational decisions? If you're not consciously working on taking risk and responsibility on decision-making, you're staying in your comfort zone. Subordinates look to leaders to make decisions. The success of the decision, however, doesn't lie in the decision itself alone. Let's say I made a really good decision to sign up to the gym. However, I never go, therefore don't receive the benefits. Was that a good decision after all? The key to successful decision-making is what happens after a decision is made. On a project, a project manager may have selected the wrong subcontractor. However, there is ample opportunity along the way to make additional decisions which can still yield positive outcomes. The ability to make decisions work is what attracts the remuneration but also the right to lead. Most people don't implement decisions long enough for them to be successful. Just look at how many gym memberships are purchased in January comparative to the attendance rate come March. When we're looking at decision-making, even indecision is a decision. Making decisions so as to not spread frustration and uncertainty also falls back onto the Triple E leader to develop foresight, which is why having vision and the developed ability of the muscle in your mind to exercise foresight is imperative. Being able to anticipate outcomes and logical consequences ensures that a decision is made. Sometimes when a decision needs to be made, people are sent down the path of collecting more information, but that is also a form of indecision at times. It's the indecision which causes a breakdown in communication and trust, and people start to speculate and generate their own ideas in waiting for a decision. And certainly, on project delivery, indecision costs money. Each day that a contractor waits for direction is money. Each day that an issue isn't resolved onsite is money. There are tangible and intangible consequences from not making a decision, so ensure it's all quantified as you may sit there in indecision. Projects have to move forward. Businesses have to move forward. If they're not moving forward, they're sliding backwards. The one certain rule of every single project is it will be finished at some point. The question is, when?

Where do most people falter, though, when it comes to decision-making? It's the fear of failure. They fear that if course A is selected, it's wrong, and it should have been B all along. Remember, the success of the decision lies in the implementation, not the initial decision. This fear of failure plays out on the macro and micro in lives all the time, and it holds people back. Failure is accepted only when an individual has done their absolute best. If they haven't, then there is no justification for failure.

Here's what Courtemanche has to say when asked to give advice to aspiring leaders about moving forward with decisions: 'The difference between people that succeed and people who don't succeed, is that people who succeed are willing to make decisions, move quickly and fail. So, it's important to have a culture where failure is not only accepted, but is actually celebrated because it means that you have forward momentum and you're learning. Really, there's a direct correlation between success and people that are able to move fast and make decisions as opposed to people who sit around and over-pontificate and over-talk. The difference between entrepreneurs and non-entrepreneurs, in my mind, is oversimplification – it's the difference between people who are willing to take a risk, put the resources behind it, and actually do something as opposed to just talk about it. That's really what the difference is. You see an opportunity, you're willing to put your livelihood at risk and put your resources at work, and you're willing to get up every single day and fight for that idea until you see the success. I think that's one of those things that you just have to do. Make decisions, move fast. Don't be afraid to fail. Failure is not failure, it's learning, and then you just keep going until you succeed.'

FOCUS ON THE PRIORITIES

'Time management is an oxymoron. Time is beyond our control, and the clock keeps ticking regardless of how we lead our lives. Priority management is the answer to maximising the time we have.' **– John C Maxwell**

A source of frustration for anyone on teams, from cadets to subcontractors to business leaders and stakeholders – is when the priorities aren't clear. At the same time, those carrying out the work may not have the sensitivity for what is urgent and important, versus not urgent and certainly not important. Within my own business, this is something that I've had to learn and be disciplined with. I'm a visionary, and I know that when I conceive a new idea, I want to see it come into fruition as soon as I can. I've learnt that a 'no' is just a 'not yet', and that stringent parameters about how I use my time to get the greatest results are required. If I'm not having a narrow focus on the priorities, then I also can't expect others to focus on theirs. Especially on projects, there will always be something that comes up, but leaders need to have a heightened sensitivity as to what warrants their time and response, between 'right now' and 'I can get to this later'. If you're not all-in on the priorities and picking low-hanging fruit, those around you will follow suit, and you'll find it more cumbersome than it needs to be to get outcomes. It may seem obvious that a focus needs to be on the priorities, but I've had senior leadership question the status of the window coverings package before the structure was completed when working on project delivery. So no, what seems common practice is not common at all. Having a focus on priorities also stems from being time sensitive. Time is my highest value and there is nothing that irks me more than wasted time. I'm personally grateful that this sensitivity for time has always been core to me, and that I make decisions from the perspective of time first. Once it's gone, it's not coming back. And whilst many understand this on an intellectual level, they don't truly embody this as their actions say otherwise. Assuredly, if someone is lax and complacent with the time of others, I don't want to know how they while theirs away.

To manage priorities first requires consciousness as to what you can control and what you can't control, which informs what warrants a reaction, or otherwise. Rooney explains, 'There's a business principle about the locus of control and influence, and a beautiful diagram where one circle sits inside another. The more you focus on the things you can control, the more that circle grows. If you spend all your time worrying about what everyone else should do, your circle of control diminishes because you're not spending any time enacting the change you can. Now, that theory is enormously similar to the serenity prayer that my nana used to have embroidered on the wall, which is, *Grant me the serenity to accept the things I cannot change, courage to change the things I can, and wisdom to know the difference.*' A level of flexibility and ability to rearrange competing priorities is valuable, especially in dynamic environments like construction. Just because one thing is a priority to another person or party, that doesn't mean it automatically becomes an immediate priority to you.

'As you become more astute at ascertaining priorities, you'll become better at knowing when you can push back on certain things,' reflects Russo. You need to know, and also act on, what you can delegate to others, whether that is upstream or downstream. Russo continues that, 'At times, you need to do really long hours and put in extra effort to get through your work activities. I think those competing demands become the new norm as a leader. Prioritisation is a professional competency that you need to develop the same as when you start out, you might need to learn how to use a computer or get really good at using MS Word or Excel. As you get further in your career, you need to get really good at prioritisation, and it's going to be a key strength.' This would have to be the biggest bridge micromanagers need to cross when aspiring to leadership positions. Learning the difference between high-value tasks and low-value tasks is imperative, as the organisation or project that you're with isn't getting the greatest value out of a leader who is doing document control.

Prioritisation isn't only limited to the workplace. I'm very strict with my priorities inside and outside of business, and know the value of my time. Like Slattery, I outsource. 'You can't do everything! I'm a big believer in outsourcing in my personal life, I don't want to spend my weekends and family time doing tasks that others do better than me. It doesn't make sense. Put your energy into what you do best.'

What happens to a business or project if the leader doesn't set the priorities? By not doing this, you're negating the essence of this chapter, which is getting the best out of others. The outcomes and results are compromised when a leader doesn't prioritise and steer the ship in the right direction. It benefits no-one. The overall performance of people suffers. Who can move forward with conviction when there is no clarity? Russo comments that, 'In the worst cases, if there is that leadership void, teams may not work to a clear goal and instead may meander and therefore really not either deliver for themselves or for the client, and potentially the business is at risk if they develop something that is contrary to the objectives set out to begin with.' In every situation though, there can be opportunity for those who see it. 'Sometimes a void of leadership can be a great thing, it can create the next generation of leaders and oftentimes someone will step up into the role and do a fantastic job of it. That's a great opportunity for that person, whoever it may be. Ideally, that's done with a bit of strategic support and not just that accidental absence,' observes Russo.

To even know what the priorities are requires a dedicated amount of pre-planning and preparedness. Again, it may sound simple to do, but go and ask people around you after you've read this how much of their day is consistently dedicated to planning versus execution and being proactive rather than reactionary. I am convinced that the number of meetings would be dramatically reduced if most people planned. As Nathan reflected on his leadership journey, he consistently attests his successes to planning and preparedness. 'My lack of experience was made up for by my preparation because I would go into meetings or I'd be onsite at 6:30am the next morning, and I would be a couple of steps ahead of people because I'd done the work. I'd prepared and I knew exactly what I had to do. These are things that I think set people aside. We're seeing this in our business now. We're seeing people in their mid-twenties who will be future leaders in our industry, and certainly, we hope will be leaders in our business. Watching these young men and women commit to the work and prepare and think about things and ask questions ... You were prepared not because you're so intelligent or you're so knowledgeable that you knew everything, you're prepared because you'd done the work.'

Being prepared is simply great personal and business leadership, and a Triple E leader who is consistently ready is one who will be able to weather the rough seas and storms that undoubtedly come. Demonstrating this is also reflective of the ability to have foresight, by looking into the environment ahead – even if it's two or three steps ahead – and implementing appropriate controls to ensure desired actions unfold. It demonstrates thinking, and we've ascertained that thinking is not very common. Having a level of flexibility and agility is equally as imperative, as being creative as situations unfold is invaluable to problem resolution. No plan should be followed blindly or without checking for its relevancy. Embodying this trait ensures that a Triple E leader makes success of the outcome their personal responsibility and isn't sitting around waiting for things to happen; they make it happen.

CHAPTER FIVE

THEIR SUCCESS

SET THEM UP FOR SUCCESS

'You have not lived today until you have done something for someone who can never repay you.' – **John Bunyan**

Leadership tools cannot be applied without any discretion to any scenario and expect the same outcomes. Part of being a leader is knowing what tools, strategies and tactics to use at any given time based on the individual and situation at hand in a measured and controlled way. A leader needs to look at the personalities, attributes and natural dispositions of the individual, and ensure that within an organisation they are actually set up for success; that they are given every opportunity to flex their natural talents and play to their strengths. Understanding everyone's differences and seeing someone for their individuality is very important for a leader, as you can't assume that the same tactics have a uniform approach. It's irrational to expect a person who loves dealing with people and being in conversation to be holed up doing highly technical work with little to no people involvement. At the same time, there are people who love being behind a screen with plans and numbers, and have no business dealing with clients directly. Setting them up for success doesn't mean looking after each individual's happiness. It's not the responsibility of a leader to make a subordinate happy. Happiness is an inside job and only the individual has that onus. But it does mean that as a leader, you not only have the right people on the right projects, but they're also in the right role on that project. A leader needs to provide the operating environment for success in the first instance, and not have all the cards stacked up against someone that they're leading.

Before my own journey of enlightenment to understanding my person and natural disposition, I was put to work on a project that very quickly unfolded to be a hellhole for me, both in terms of the people and the project. It was turmoil, because 100% of the work that I was tasked with and in the environment that it had to be done in was a personal and professional nightmare for me. Everything that I loved and thrived on doing was replaced with precisely what I didn't love for a client and a cause that I didn't believe in. Everything suffered as a result, including my outputs and my own sanity and wellbeing. I cannot use the term leadership in this application, but even as managers, forcing your subordinates to perform by shoving the same work down their throat is not how to extract superior performance. It's one of the times where I failed myself for staying too long in places I shouldn't have, because I still hadn't constructed myself to be able to see how out of alignment this situation was. Despite the living nightmare that this project unfolded to from every perspective, I'm grateful that it happened, because it was the rude awakening I needed to take back agency over my own career and ensure that I will never be at the behest of inadequate management in order to have a career in construction. I was able to turn the horror into rocket fuel to fire my dreams and real ambitions. I share this affliction with you in reflection of the responsibility of Triple E leaders to set your people up for success. The aforementioned is not an isolated case. It happens all the time in this industry: people are put to carry out roles that aren't in alignment with what they are best at or love doing (it's accepted that just about no-one can ever carry out 100% of the work that they love, but 70% is much better than 10%), they're not given clear development pathways or expectations, and are rarely seen and heard for their natural disposition but rather as a simple resource. At the time, I didn't know myself well enough to articulate why this project wasn't working for me. It didn't make sense to me then to go from loving what I do, to hating every waking minute of it ferociously. But as a Triple E leader, if someone is floundering and not thriving, you don't beat them with a stick and say it's their fault. There's always a reason behind a change in performance, and you need to find out why, so you can set them up for success and enable their best performance.

What this requires from a Triple E leader is foresight. One of the most powerful things you can ever do for a person is to *see* them. Not just for who they are today, and certainly not in the container that is the physical self they come in, but for who they can be. My mentor, Ron Malhotra, *saw* me. Well before I could see even a fragment of who I am today, and also whilst my own foresight was being developed, Ron saw my unique composition and what would align with me, so that success could be aligned, organic and I would flow with it. Ron worked with me to specifically craft environments in which I would thrive, creative ventures which would allow the greatest impact to those who come in contact with it. This is one of the highest expressions of Triple E leadership. When you can see people for all of who they are, then they also need the space to bring their whole person to work.

Adra has the mission of helping people become a better version of themselves, which has informed his vision at Mossman to build the people who build the homes. 'When we implemented that vision into the business and we started empowering our staff and making sure that they were achieving what their life goals are within our business, that's when we started to see true success and that's what success is to me.'

As I was writing this book, I ran a poll on my LinkedIn asking if people in my community feel that they have to leave themselves at the door when they go into work. 51% voted that they do. It's diminishing for people to leave their sense of self at home when they go into work. Like waves hitting a cliff shore, this is one of the ways in which people lose their identity and sense of self-expression, as they've been made to feel that there's no space for their person in the workplace. I know, because that's what happened to me – as I shared at the start of the book. It was suffocating and debilitating at best, but I was conscious to it. I asked Slattery what she thought were the key considerations of leading people. Her response was premised on the same: 'It is so important that people can bring their whole selves to work. This allows them to be their best self, innovate and demonstrate peak productivity. When I started out, I had interests outside the business – music, art, architecture. Whilst architecture was aligned with the industry, I saw my other passions as things that had to be kept completely separate. Over time I've realised that it's possible to carry all parts of yourself into your professional career, and that those around you and the wider community benefit when you do.' Only people who don't know who they are themselves are intimidated by others who bring their whole person to work.

Only when you truly see an individual and can identify more of what they should be doing that's in alignment with their person, does your immense foresight and emotional intelligence come into play. 'It's much more productive to strengthen a strength than strengthen a weakness,' recalls Slattery. 'Everyone has something to offer, and by focusing on people's strengths, and listening to where they see themselves and what they value, alignment and a common vision is created.'

In his book, *Good to Great*, Jim Collins extensively details the importance of not just having the right people on the bus with you, it's having the right people in the right seats. But it takes the vision of a leader to see an individual to put them in the right seat first. 'The other thing is, there's oftentimes a misalignment from a leader's expectation of where a person is and where they can be, and that individual's ambitions and expectations of where they are and where they can be. They both could be less or more in either direction,' recalls Abraham. 'You actually have to love people. You're going to look at them and you have to say, *There is something great about everybody*. As I said, they would not have been employed by Hickory if they weren't intelligent and capable, and there are a number of great features about them. All right, we've ticked all those boxes. It means they're capable. You just have to be able to find and then stroke their potential. I don't think you can read that in a book anywhere. You have to listen to people; you have to find what they need. Then your mind has to be very clear and open about what opportunities your business currently has to be able to slot them in a place that lets them grow. We've had cases where we've had general foremen that we've been at our wit's end about due to their non-performance and how to get them to improve and get what we want out of them. Then, all of a sudden, we've thought outside the square and we've had an opportunity that's available for them. Then when you put them in, they do absolutely brilliant. You look in and say, *Look at that. We were about to offer that person a redundancy a few months ago and look at what we have now*. It's a difficult thing to do to throw someone in the scrap heap, when there was a point in time that you thought they were good enough to employ. I think that everybody has potential. It's incumbent on us to try and find how to get it out of them. What paddock do you have to put them in to let them grow?'

'Human beings are not things needing to be motivated and controlled. They are four-dimensional: body, mind, heart and spirit.' – **Stephen Covey**

This is where a heart-set, not just mindset, comes into play, because to achieve the above you need to have a genuine curiosity for your followers. The most dangerous thing you can do when it comes to leading others is to make an assumption based on your own preconceived notions and dispositions. Slattery also credits curiosity as fundamental for success. 'It is crucial to take a genuine interest in those you're leading. What do they love doing? What excites and motivates them? Everyone is so multifaceted, and you really need to listen and consider their experiences, what might scare them or hold them back. Only they can tell you their ambitions, but sometimes an outsider's perspective can reveal what's getting in the way of their potential.'

Mirams also shared that she responds to every message she gets on LinkedIn, to the surprise of many who didn't think she would respond. Why? Because she has genuine care for her people. It's not always the grandest gestures which reverberate the furthest. When was the last time you asked deep and meaningful questions to your subordinates that had nothing to do with football or their weekend? When was the last time you went out of your way to ensure that someone else would succeed – whether in their role, as your client and so on? When was the last time you truly cared whether someone would achieve what they wanted or not? When was the last time *you* set someone *else* up for success?

You see, no-one will care until they know how much you do. I didn't want to use the term empathy when discussing the emotional aspect of leadership, as solely being empathetic can leave others in the exact same place. For example (situational dependent), if you over-empathise with an individual, are you justifying and validating their excuses and limitations? If you are truly a leader that is focused on extracting others' potential and performance, empathy isn't what you lead with. You can be a heart-driven leader, but that requires delivering the hard truths and holding the mirror for what others don't necessarily want to hear or see. The balance is having both relatability but also credibility – you're human to relate to the situation, but your credibility comes in so you can lead them forward. When I mentor others, I'm the first to celebrate their wins, but I'm also the first to call them out when they believe their excuses and limitations more than anything else – especially if they're blaming external circumstances and events. If you are constantly at the behest of external conditions, what are you in control of? Nothing. Whilst you can extend heart lines and a deep and genuine care for who you are leading, being truly empathetic is about making decisions, giving feedback or having conversations that are in their best interest and not just what they want to hear.

To Adra, empathy is, 'Understanding why people act the way they do. Why people say what they say. Understanding how to read people and understanding an outcome in a much better way, instead of looking at a situation or person I'm dealing with in a negative way immediately and being irrational. That's probably helped me the most in that sense, because I look at things and stop and think about them before I react to absolutely any of that. Don't get me wrong, there are times when we're irrational. We do act in a bad way, but that's obviously everybody and we're humans and we can do that. 90% of the time is me stepping back in a situation, understanding and having empathy on why it became what it did. That's pretty much what's helped me understand and accept things that happen in life.' It's an art and a science of a conversation, and a very delicate line to walk when learning how to have these conversations of extending a heart line, whilst holding your own leadership authority, and understanding the root cause of a situation that isn't marred in emotions. Remember, no-one said leadership was easy.

LET THEM LEAD

'People want guidance, not rhetoric; they need to know what the plan of action is and how it will be implemented. They want to be given responsibility to help solve the problem and the authority to act on it.' – **Howard Schultz**

A marker of a confident leader and one sure of their own authority, is when they get out of the way and let others lead. This doesn't look like making someone responsible for an outcome by sending them forth with handcuffs and constantly breathing down their neck, second-guessing their every move. Over time, that has the ability to erode the confidence in people that interact with you, setting them up for long-term failure, not success. That's a stifling environment, and also formally known as micromanagement. This is where the higher intelligence of a Triple E leader needs to be developed, as they need to know when to lead and when to let others lead. You're not adequately managing your own genius and capacity if you are constantly in the way of others doing what you charged them with. A key part of Slattery's leadership philosophy is the notion of 'here if you need', adapted from the world of netball. This involves having confidence in her leadership by knowing that her team have got it and she'll be there if they need her. 'If I ask how I can help, I may be asked to speak to a certain client, review a cost plan or advise on a fee variation, so I'll do this while trying to stay focused on helping exactly how they've asked me to.' Slattery also discussed her belief that those not commonly involved in management often demonstrate their leadership abilities as soon as they are given the opportunity. 'At Slattery we look at leadership as something that can be done by anyone at any level. Whilst the title is one thing, we have students that lead other students or guide the entire office on IT implementation or a Thought Leadership piece. Leadership and seniority are not synonyms.'

It is worth differentiating between management and leadership. Not everyone needs to be a leader or wants to be, as organisations and projects also need brilliant managers. Management deals with the administrative and implementation side of an organisation, with a prime focus on the execution of key tasks and functions. Take a project manager, who is tasked with delivery of a key function of a construction business – delivering projects. Just because they're at the helm of a project, doesn't automatically equate to leadership. A key difference between the two functions is the arena of focus. Russo, who is charged with leading many project managers, reflects on the difference: 'Management is a stepping stone to leadership, obviously, but equally I don't think all managers will necessarily become leaders. I think leaders that emerge from management ranks are those that are willing to make difficult decisions. The ones that are willing to admit mistakes, the ones that understand that respect needs to be earned as opposed to those that demand respect. There's a very significant difference. As much as there's lots of leadership training and courses, there are some attributes to leadership that seem to come more naturally to some people than others. It's usually the defining piece of leadership, but it's making those difficult human decisions that often separate leaders from managers.'

I like the simple perspective Colin Powell, retired general, summarised, 'Managers can be leaders, but leaders should not be managers.'

Not letting others lead also stifles critical and innovative thinking, creating people around you who don't have dynamic thinking and are constantly relying on you for every single solution. This is not in the best interest of setting others up for success, as it's disabling rather than enabling. 'Everyone we employ is a capable, intelligent person. They are oftentimes capable of resolving matters themselves with a little more time. You need to let that be. Sometimes we're young and ambitious and we have a lot of dignity and pride, and we feel we have to be at the front of every thought, decision or problem – I've learned very quickly that I don't actually. That's going to no doubt help me with my sanity and blood pressure in the future. For me, as an individual, one of my biggest learnings is what patience actually means. Things are allowed to resolve themselves with a bit of time,' reflects Abraham. Let people sit with a problem and go through their own thinking processes to resolve it. If you jump in too quickly, you're not allowing them a chance to build these mental pathways and processes so that next time, when an issue comes up, they can come to their own conclusion. When I get a call from a client, I know that at times they just want a simple direction from me. But it's a disservice to them if I just give them an answer. I would rather spend more time with them now to give them mental frameworks, guide them through the situation, send them away with things to consider, and come back to me with their response. When they detail their thinking process to me and I can see the rationale and how they came to their conclusion, I've set them up for success as they're learning to lead themselves and have confidence in their own abilities.

'The function of leadership is to produce more leaders, not more followers.' – **Ralph Nadar**

But what does letting others lead enable a leader to do? You're not wrong if your immediate answer was to develop other leaders, which is a simple necessity. It's to create a loyal followership. A Triple E leader has Triple E followers. When a Triple E leader is able to let others lead, they're also demonstrating what brilliant followership looks like. The strength of your authority and power as a leader is going to be reflected in who is following you. The way to attract brilliance is by being brilliant. Letting others lead generates two very powerful forces in followership: respect and loyalty. 'I don't think respect can be overstated,' says Rooney. 'Leadership with a capital L is talked about a lot, but we never talk about followership … What do we need to do to support people that allow you to lead them? I think, as a leader, it's really important to show people the strategy. Where is the lighthouse we're all heading towards? Then break it down into a number of areas so people can gain comfort in what's expected of them, and importantly, create space for their growth and improvement over time. I think it's a real yin and yang balance.' As a leader, you also need to be extremely stringent as to where your time and effort is going. You don't need to jump into every single situation, spreading yourself way too thin and not focusing on the horizon. To lead you need to free yourself up, so learn when to lead and when to let others lead.

BUILDING RELATIONSHIPS

'People don't care how much you know until they know how much you care.' – **Theodore Roosevelt**

I cannot speak for other industries, but the construction industry is built off relationships. Anything from ventures, collaborations, opportunities and promotions are premised on relationships. What do you think will get you further – relationship equity or financial equity? Think of building your relationship equity as making deposits in a bank. You continually need to make deposits into your relationships before you can make a withdrawal. If you try to withdraw too soon, there may not be enough. There is no antidote or fast way of doing this. The fastest way is actually via a slow burn, and no-one really wants to do that, because it takes a lot of time and there are no immediate results. I invested the first seven years of my career (ongoing) in the industry tending to my network and never making a withdrawal – only deposits. Building relationships also stems from a genuine care and consideration for the other person and the people in your community or organisation. And this goes beyond the superficial interest in what someone did on the weekend or how their football game went. Controversial in the construction industry, I know. That doesn't deeply connect or convert. Relationships that are developed purely out of intellect will not withstand the test of time, nor when the seas get rough in the industry, and they do.

Triple E leaders are cognisant that at the centre of all their efforts are people. There is just about nothing that I can do for and in my business that is isolated without building relationships. But to do that, I must have a deep understanding, appreciation and consideration for the people that I am leading. A curiosity for others cannot be manufactured, it has to be genuine. Surely you can think of times when someone was trying to take an interest in your life but only for it to feel perfunctory. Ask really considerate questions, truly listen not just to what is being said but to what isn't being said and develop a mutual commitment to each other. When you do this, as a leader, what you are able to tap into is *insight*. Maybe there are deep-rooted cultural issues on a project that no-one really wants to come forth on – relationships will give you that insight. Relationships will give you honest and timely feedback on tenders. Without relationship equity, your followership and the stakeholders around you won't go the extra mile for you, they won't share the hard truths with you, they won't partner with you to win either.

When Mirams was asked what someone would need to start learning and doing right now in order to give her a run for her money, she said, 'I think the most important thing is to have really great relationships. This is a very small industry and relationships are really important. I have worked very hard on relationships my whole career, and the support we have received from our subcontractors is incredible and it's due to the relationships that the executive team have had with the subcontractors for our entire careers. Some of mine go back to 1998 – so I'd say relationships.'

Trust is one of the currencies you can transact in, come building relationships, and it's a currency that transgresses any job title, experience or leverage from a company name. Before you can expect others to trust you, ask yourself – do you even trust yourself? According to Stephen M.R. Covey, former president and CEO of Covey Leadership Centre, research shows that only 51% of employees trust senior management, and only 28% believe CEOs are a credible source of information. You simply cannot be a Triple E leader without strategically generating trust. First it has to be earned, and then carefully tended to over time. Your title or years of experience don't get you trust; it's earned and can be destroyed in an instance. To get to the top of any game, a person has to have earned the trust of a lot of people along the way, and also tended to keep that trust. That's no easy feat, when you really consider all the nuances involved, and the consistency in character that's required.

Adra shares a similar sentiment: 'Through my years of business, one of the good things I've done is network with a lot of people. That trust I had built with these people just helped me grow very, very quickly. In our first year of business, we turned over $4 million.'

The thing about trust is that no-one will just tell you that they don't trust you, it shows up in their behaviours, actions and outcomes around you. It was Russo's leadership proposition of building genuine relationships in the industry which drew me in the first place. He reflects on the value of this in relationships: 'Relationships and the way teams work are critical to project success. By that I don't just mean relationships where people say, *Dave is a great guy and he's good to go out and have a coffee with.* Professional relationships require, certainly, that you need to get along on a personal level, but more importantly they need to be founded in trust. That you can do the job that you're paid to deliver on. The track record is what I value.' Russo continues to reflect on how trust is generated: 'If I say I'm going to do something, I make sure I see it through and deliver on it. That's certainly the basis for my relationships and how they've been built. Like any good thing, it takes a long time to build those. It doesn't just happen. It's not a flick of a switch either, and it's not that they [relationships] weren't there one day and they were the next. It's just something that's evolved over my career. It's about just maintaining contact. If you form genuine relationships, you should, as that word says, be genuine.'

You cannot break trust with people and continue to influence them, nor can trust be built by taking shortcuts, because trust is generated through results, not because you said you'll do something. We see a lot of subpar leadership thinking of trust as an elastic band, in that it can be stretched to no end. John Maxwell reflects that trust is built by consistent exemplification of competence, character and connection. What we see frequently in the corporate world are lapses of character, because again, people don't know who they are. You cannot expect your followership to simply trust you, the onus is not on them to give it to you, but for you to generate it and strategically construct it. And don't think you can stretch it too much, because it may just snap. As Stephen Covey said, 'Trust is the glue of life. It's the most essential ingredient in effective communication. It's the foundational principle that holds all relationships.'

A commonality that I see with industry professionals is that most will only do something when there's an immediate need for it. For example, 2020 saw many redundancies, and only then did people start scraping around for a network. A little too late. Building relationships is akin to farming – you toil, plough, sow and only harvest at the end. 'Relationships shouldn't just be nurtured when it suits you, when you might be targeting a particular project, you should be having those relationships all the time. That genuine interest in what's happening with that particular person or organisation at any point in time, whether you're working with them or not working with them,' says Russo. A Triple E leader constantly tends to relationships without expecting anything in return, because they know they're not owed or promised anything for their efforts. When you tie in a genuine curiosity for others with a deep desire to add value, then this isn't difficult to do at all.

I asked Courtemanche what he thought the real relationship between developing connections and leadership was. He commented that, 'One can't exist without the other. The construction industry is wholly dependent upon how effectively its members can connect and communicate with each other, and leadership is no different.' It's your duty as a Triple E leader to not just develop broad relationships, but also generate depth, which is where the greatest leaders display the ability to connect.

In the hyper-connected social age that we live in, people can actually be left feeling more disconnected, which is why connection is the new currency. However the connection is facilitated, it needs to be facilitated. People need a sense of belonging and to feel connected to something outside of themselves – it's simply a fundamental human desire. Why else would social media attach people to the screen like it does? It's to manufacture connectivity. But let's take it to construction: 'In construction, you have all the different trades coming together, along with architects, engineers, contractors, owners, material equipment suppliers, banks, lenders and insurers. How in the world are you going to be successful if you don't have people working off the same set of information, and showing up at the right time at the right job site with the right materials and the right equipment – all of that requires connection. There's a direct correlation between projects that are successful and the ability of those teams to connect and build high levels of trust. In my years building Procore and getting to know stakeholders up, down and through the construction trade, I've found this correlation to be indisputable. Why would you do it any other way?' reflects Courtemanche on the concept of digitisation and connectivity, to bring everyone together, build that trust and maintain high levels of connectivity. Regardless of the tool used, what needs to matter in the eye of a Triple E leader is facilitating the high levels of connection.

Conclusively, when it comes to building relationships, is transparency. I've worked on projects where nine out of ten conversations were closed door. I've also worked on projects where I was privy to anything I desired to know. This isn't to say everyone at every level needs to be privy to all that is going on, that will just clog communication channels. But it is the transparency that leans into generating the aforementioned trust. The Australian Leadership Index conducted a national survey and found that the more institutional leaders are perceived as transparent, the more they are perceived to show leadership for the greater good. However, within the private sector, national businesses and multinational corporations are viewed by 21% and 20% of respondents, respectively, as transparent to a 'fairly large' or 'extremely large' extent. That's not much. When you are transparent in your plans and objectives, you have a higher chance of connecting your mission and vision with that of the people who are in your team or community. I've learnt from my mentor the value of showing people what's happening in the business. There's no need for a smokescreen or to dance around situations. People really don't appreciate that, which usually occurs under a guise of following policies. Abraham shares a similar sentiment; 'It's really important to be transparent as a manager and a leader. You need to be candid. I don't want to use the word honest because you can be honest without being transparent and still withhold information, I find that if you can do that with your people, it builds intimacy and trust, which is the very foundation of good communication in an organisation. That's the style.'

HIGH PERFORMANCE

'You don't get any medal for trying something, you get medals for results.' – **Bill Parcells**

You can show someone the world, expand their world of possibilities and take them through a journey of alternative futures. But then what? Sitting and dreaming of what could be is expansive and formative, but this needs to be rendered with action. The grandest of plans and actions are certainly not worth the paper they're written on without execution. Eliciting people into action is a fundamental aspect of leadership, and this is recognised as performance. You can look to the history of leadership and see that the greatest leaders have been able to extract the best performance out of people that have interacted with them. If your project or business isn't running at optimum levels of performance, the leader hasn't been able to extract the best out of their subordinates. Remember, there's a distinction here; it's not about getting the *most* out of people, it's about getting the *best* out of people – sometimes the most is the best. And to achieve results, you need people to bring their best. Can you expect someone to bring their best if they see that you, as a leader, aren't? As the opening quote of this chapter said, you won't get any awards or accolades for trying. As a leader, you're on stage for the results that you have been able to extract from others, and yourself, because at the end of the day, leadership is about delivering value to your people. It's being the person who has had enough with the status quo and wants to be the one to get things done. No-one said that this was an easy venture – nothing worth having or doing is easy. To achieve such high performance requires an obsessive and fierce commitment to it. Leaders make an empirical difference in the performance of others, reflecting on the military philosophy that there are no such things as bad teams, only bad leaders.

To extract best performance is also to have and live in accordance with high standards. If you look behind the facade, most people don't have high standards congruently in each arena of their life. They are passive with everything. Triple E leaders reject mediocrity, which is a disease in society. It has infiltrated the minds of the masses to cap their performance and potential. Triple E leaders only subscribe to excellent, exceptional and exemplary standards. Have you wondered why people have lost their ways, and as such, their standards? It is truly of recent times that we are witnessing a very sharp and rapid decline of standards. Take a moment to look around and sincerely analyse where you see the application of high standards. This certainly leans into the discourse on values, where most people aren't living a principle-based approach in accordance with the higher values of humanity. You may hold yourself to high standards, but how do you hold others to high standards all the same? First, when you make it clear that this is the play, you won't be attracting people of a lesser calibre of mind. But then, it's about shifting the focus to the results that you want, and the certain performance metrics and outputs that you are expecting. You need to be very descript and clear as to what brilliant looks like for you, then let people get on with it. For three months of printing my first book, I sent it back multiple times because the spine was millimetres out. To some, it would have been 'good enough'. For me, it wasn't. This doesn't just apply to the professional self. Personally, I have always carried myself to high standards, but for a very long time I would drop that standard in order to be more accommodating of others. What that left me with was a reduced sense of self. It's not your duty as a leader to drop your standards and expectations to meet others. It's your duty to demand others raise their standards to meet yours. The culmination of people dropping their standards is precisely what has allowed mediocrity to be accepted and have permeated all too many corners of the industry. As a Triple E leader, you don't have to feel a sense of obligation to put up with the excuses and limitations of others. If you do that, you're reaffirming the status quo.

A key marker of high performance is resourcefulness. It's not feasible as a leader to attempt to do everything ourselves. When I proceed with any new venture, I immediately assess what I will do, and what I will outsource. This is mobilisation of resources, and being continually aware of what I do have at my disposal and maximising that. Remember that there may be a shortage of resources, but not a shortage of resourcefulness. There is no cap to ingenuity. Mirams, as a high-performance person herself was asked what the language of high-performance sounds like. She reflected, 'I'm not good when staff say, *You can't know, it won't work.* I like to hear people say, *That's a challenge. That's an opportunity, but we've got these issues with it.* Just keep an open mind. That's all people need to do. It's not any harder than that. Just keep an open mind and don't shut down very quickly.' Most people are wired to think about why something won't work, instead of critically thinking as to how something can work, or even better, how they could make it work. Both personally and professionally, think to yourself, *For how much longer can I live with my self-imposed limitations?* The greatest outcomes, companies, solutions and movements are a product of someone making it work and driving a vision to completion.

But what is the exact cocktail of high-performance attributes? How can you, as a leader, start to recognise this within others, as to ensure that this is who you are surrounding yourself with? Nathan is recognised in the industry as banding together high-performance teams. When reflecting on the high-performance profile of people he hires, he says, 'Values and work ethic, to us, are more important. People that have a level of tenacity, they're committed to what they do. They have a strong level of integrity. Are they consistent, trustworthy people? All those things, I think, make for great performance people. You can have the smartest person in the room, but if they're not prepared to apply themselves or they're thinking about the next step before they've even taken this step, they're probably not the people that we're after. I think people that are really focused that do the hard work and are prepared for what they have to do, matter. I think there needs to be some problem-solving ability and ability to apply learning to given situations.' Ambition within individuals cannot be taught, but when you do find that person with ambition, it's your duty as a leader to guide and direct that performance and not quell it.

Leaders need to be highly aware that A-players only want to be surrounded by other A-players. There's a certain synergy that is created when A-players meet A-players – there's nothing they can't make come into fruition. If Triple E leaders tolerate poor performance from others, the high-performing players are bound to leave the team. This is a reflection of the inconsistency in character of the leader and what standards they accept. This is reflective of Russo's ideology on high performance: 'I think, with very few exceptions, high performance is very much individually driven and if you surround high performers with other high performers there is just a natural level that those individuals display which gathers momentum and you get more and more high performance across the broader team. I think, for the most part, and certainly from what I've seen, high performers generally take care of themselves. The one thing you need to do as a leader is where you get that underperformer, identify that quickly and be seen to be decisive around dealing with underperformance within the workplace, so that high performers continue what they're doing and realise that how they go about their work is actually valued and appreciated.' As you're reading this paragraph, reflect back to the paragraph on the quality of your followership. It speaks volumes about you as a leader if you have generated a deep sense of loyalty that automatically drives high performance in your A-players. Have these types of people in your corner, and you, as a leader, can just about make anything come into fruition.

As Triple E leaders, though, you need to be cognisant that people don't come ready-made. When I first met Ron Malhotra, I wasn't even a shadow of the person I am today. Whilst I am cut from the same fabric and possessed all the right attributes to achieve greatness, I didn't start off like this. To get me to where I am today took serious investment from Ron, and me, of course, brought my level of serious effort to match his. Generating brilliant performance from others takes time, even if they have the right alchemy of attributes. That's why the nuanced art and science of being able to mentor and coach others is a desirable attribute of Triple E leaders. I say desirable, because if you look to the likes of Steve Jobs, this wasn't something he was known for doing, but he was exceptional.

When Abraham was asked how he's been able to mentor others, he says, 'You have to look at an individual from all angles. You have to really try to empathise or understand – what background did they come from? What are their limitations? What scares them? What holds them back? Only they can tell you what their ambitions are, but sometimes they can't see that there might be other factors in their life that prevent them from getting their ambition. There is the methodical management 101 method of performance reviews, goal setting and monitoring how you're going with all of that. I think that's really boring but I think it works. It certainly worked for me through my career because I had really great leaders and mentors. If you're just relying on that, then I think you can leave some opportunities on the table.' To truly bring out the best *performance* and *potential,* being a Triple E mentor is only going to be to your benefit, and to those around you.

PART THREE

CONSTRUCTING PROJECTS

CHAPTER SIX
OUR ENTERPRISE

Before we move into the last phase of your leadership construction, let's recap what we have covered so far. Constructing You is leadership of you, as you cannot lead others if you haven't first led yourself. Constructing Others is leadership of one to a collective, where you gained key insights and principles into what's required to bring people along the journey with you into your vision and also what you need in your toolbox to bring out the best in others. Now we're going to be diving into leadership at large. Constructing Projects is leadership of one to many, looking at leadership of the masses and broader organisations. This is leadership at scale. When Mirams was promoted from regional commercial manager to director at Multiplex, her boss at the time said it'll take her twelve months to change her thinking, and it took just that. To change from the immediacy of a project to thinking like a business full of projects and projecting out from anywhere between two to five years wasn't an easy thing for Mirams to do at first, but it's a core part of a CEO mindset. Triple E leadership is not just about the people, but it's about the wealth, commercial and financial objectives of a business, in the long-term. The people will help the outcome be achieved when they are connected with the right teams and vision and are also given the space to lead, as I've discussed. To lead the masses you need to be able to add more value than anyone else to the people that you're looking to serve. Adding value is how you generate wholesale change, causing permanent shifts in how individuals operate. You don't need to look further than Apple – they may not dominate market share, but they're market leaders. Instigating change on such a broad industry and organisational level is not a venture for the faint of heart, but it's what will form part of the legacy of your leadership. If you were to disappear off the face of the earth tomorrow, what would be different? What have you left behind, that if not for you, the world wouldn't be the same? These aren't questions to sound lofty, but it's to get you to start asking yourself better questions, so as to arrive at better outcomes. The basis of leadership at large is first looking at your own house and making sure that's in order: what's best for business. Business and project will be used interchangeably hereon but remains as a reference to both entities.

BEST FOR BUSINESS

'To be successful, you have to have your heart in your business, and your business in your heart.' – **Thomas Watson**

When you're adding value, what you are inherently doing is increasing the value proposition of a business or a project. Achieving commercial outcomes *is* important. We live in an economic world, and to continue delivering an impact and growing your influence requires a refined sense of business acumen to achieve that. Even Mother Theresa had to achieve commercial outcomes in order to deliver her mission. It's rumoured that, at the time, had she chosen to withdraw her savings from the Vatican, she would have made them bankrupt. So, there's no need to get righteous and say commercial outcomes aren't important, because they are. When people combine forces, a new entity is created – a business or a project. This is a new, living entity within itself with stringent requirements, and sometimes between the interactions of people, the livelihood of a project can be neglected and forgotten. When there is conflict between individuals – personal issues, a team that doesn't work well together – then projected outcomes suffer. It's negligible practice to have a business or a project fail *unless* a leader or team have done their absolute best.

What does best for business actually mean? When you are tasked with leading a business, Russo reflects that if a business leader doesn't do these three things, the project suffers: acting decisively, taking a long-term view and always acting in the best interest of the business as a whole. Russo renders this statement with an example of a difficult decision that had to be made in the best interest of the business: 'I think it was about fourteen months ago, the start of the COVID-19 pandemic, there were lots of tough decisions borne out of uncertainty, but also going back to that, thinking about the long-term view of the business and the sustainability of the business. How we were going to make sure that the business survived, so the business would still be around in twelve months' time – was our priority number one. There were lots of decisions made around that key objective.

'That meant, unfortunately, having to stand some staff down for a period of time, reducing salaries in a number of small instances across the country, having to make a couple of staff redundant. Those sorts of decisions are difficult at the best of times. It was worse, I think, the fact that we weren't able to do things face to face. We were over the phone or Zoom, and the uncertainty that the business was facing at that time, individuals were similarly facing. That was certainly a time that I remember as being really, really stressful and quite intense.'

Slattery shared a similar consideration through the pandemic: 'We decided to keep on all our team through COVID-19, even though things weren't looking great. We focused on research, benchmarking and Thought Leadership with our spare capacity. This proved to be the best decision we could've ever made, but it was difficult from a commercial perspective at the time. It meant foregoing financial reward for our owners. This was absolutely in the best interest of the company long-term, but it was tough initially.'

If you are the Triple E leader of a business, whether your own or one that you work for, there will be times when you will need to suspend your personal endeavours to do what's best for business. I must emphasise the world *temporarily*, because if it's done continuously, then your fulfilment and engagement suffers which is no benefit to anyone involved. Russo reflects of his executive leadership function, that it's become more about ensuring that the business will be around for a lot longer than we ever will be: 'There certainly seems to be a lot of expectations from staff within a business as to what the business should be doing for them. As a leader, you sometimes feel like it's always people requesting things and you are this constant provider. That can get a bit wearisome at times and you sometimes ask yourself, *Well I'm an employee as well, why aren't I asking about what I should be getting?* But you've got to separate that personal internal dialogue from what's best for business overall.' Best for business is thinking about how you can add value first, to then get what you want. That's a time-tested principle to getting whatever it is you want, and the same applies if you're doing that through the vehicle of a business.

When Rooney was asked how she balances what she wants versus what is best for business, she provided the following framework for doing so: 'When organisations go wrong, you can often trace them back to certain leaders doing what they wanted to do rather than necessarily what was best for the organisation. Organisationally, you need to set up great governance structures where key decisions are brought to debate and worked through to make sure that you're steering the ship in the right direction. There needs to be safety to challenge ideas, and to ask whether each is taking us towards our lighthouse. Being really clear about where your long-term lighthouse is provides the language and the frameworks that others will use to decide their own course and navigate their way.'

Kurzydlo shared a time when she'd invested in the growth of an individual in the business and wanted to continue to help grow and saw the potential in the person, but they chose to resign. That same person came back with a counteroffer, and Kurzydlo made the difficult decision of letting him take it, because it was best for business. It's very tough letting an individual that you've invested in walk out the door, but if the person simply demands more for doing less, then there's no alternative. Kurzydlo highlights the interesting part about how this example unfolded. The person didn't enjoy working in the company at the time and chose to go where more pay was available. However, today, they've now come back to work as a consultant for Growthbuilt. Putting the interests of the business past what has happened in the past, is a great example of leading with a best for business mindset. Your line of thinking as a Triple E leader needs to consider: *What does the business need, what can I do for it now, in six months, in two years from now?* This is a big distinction between an employee mindset, which is only focused on what they want and how they can be satisfied, versus entrepreneurial mindset, which is focused on adding value to others first, knowing that, with patience, they're inherently getting what they want in the long run.

But in order to deliver great value and lead a business, you need to understand the business you're in. During the earlier years of my career, I thought I had a great idea for the management team. But I didn't take into consideration how this would benefit the strategy and intentions of the business I was working for at the time. Needless to say, that's changed, and I've learnt a great pitch since. 'I think you need to understand the business that you're leading,' says Russo. 'You need to know it inside out, and I'm one that's really big on leaders that have a good retention of information about the business and have that information at the tip of their tongue rather than having to go back and find it. That obviously doesn't apply to everything, but certainly for the big-picture elements of the business, I think that's really important. Then what goes hand in hand with that is knowing your people and knowing your clients. Certainly, that's probably slightly different depending on whether you're a service business or a manufacturing business, for instance, but certainly in a service industry like ours, knowing your people is critically important.' If you don't know the business you're in to the macro and micro, you're also not in a position to serve it to the best of your ability. It takes time, conversation, research, inquisitiveness, observation, curiosity and developed thinking to be able to think like a business, but it is essential in the formation of a Triple E leader. Complementary to understanding the business that you're in on the macro, is understanding it on the micro. Of course, if your natural disposition as a leader isn't in marketing, you will bring someone along to facilitate that function. But you do need to have a level of mastery in that arena, so as to still provide guidance, feedback and a level of discretion to the work being done.

Adra has adopted this approach in building the businesses he has: 'The marketing, the accounts – whenever I wore that hat and did it, I made sure I mastered it before I passed it on to an employee so I could make sure that I wasn't bringing somebody in to tell me how to run my company. Always made sure I was the one in control, but don't get me wrong, every time I hired someone, they were able to teach me a lot of things. One thing I do in businesses is that whomever I hire, I make sure they can also teach me.' If you outsource something, or have someone else perform a function for the business, but you don't actually know how it needs to be done in the first place, that's a money pit. Serial entrepreneur Adra continues, 'A lot of people say you can't wear every hat, you can't be the accountant and the marketer and so on. Well, I agree sort of with that, you can't be all of them at the same time, but you can to some extent. You just have to put in the hours – and I'd be doing endless hours, seven days a week, 7am till midnight. There'd be days where I'd go forty-eight hours with no sleep, just working right through. Not a lot of people would do that, but that's their choice. What you do in your past is what sets your future. Well, that's what I did then, but I don't do that today. The people that look at me today and say I have it easy, well, I don't have it easy. I did the hard times back then. That's what has helped me achieve. I believe that everybody should master everything in their business. When I say master, it's probably too much go get a degree in accounting, but understand why it happens.'

CULTURE

'To win in the marketplace, you must first win in the workplace.' – **Doug Conant**

Culture has been overly complicated, when culture simply represents a collective mindset. Have you noticed the word culture has the word *cult* in it? And cults are known for their groupthink ways. Culture is pertinent to leadership because it starts at the head. If the culture from the top down is toxic, for example, it will infiltrate everything – even if you try and insert good value and culture in the middle, it will still be tainted from the top. The culture in a project can stymie ideas, growth and innovation, or can be the breeding ground for exactly that, allowing the project as a collective to be the best. Culture eats strategy for breakfast, and for the most immediate reflection of a leader, look to the culture. A business which has been able to generate a culture of innovation, entrepreneurial thinking and connection is Procore, and it happens to be one of the aspects that Courtemanche is most proud of: 'We pride ourselves on the people both inside of Procore and the folks that we work with in the industry. I think I am most proud of the fact that we've been able to maintain the culture at scale – and are continually focused on improving it. We actually bring our customers together in what we call Culture Academy, where we share best practices globally with our customers who want to create a competitive advantage – a real business advantage – by investing in their people. Because it's not just about what you do, it's how you do it and who you do it with.' Culture needs to be an embodiment of what Triple E leaders value the most. Courtemanche continues, 'Culture has always been my priority because if we aren't comfortable bringing our whole, authentic selves to work, we are unable to connect with or trust our teammates as meaningfully. Vulnerability requires trust, and trust requires authenticity. As leaders, it's our job to lead by example. If we bring our authentic selves to work, it gives others permission to do the same. It's important to model showing personal vulnerabilities. This allows us to find others with strengths that are complementary to our weaknesses, gives others the chance to shine, and that ultimately makes the whole company stronger.'

Not every culture needs to be a family one, or a high-performance one, because everyone carries a different set of values and standards of what's acceptable. But whichever it is, it needs to be clearly articulated, demonstrated and upheld. It permeates every aspect of business, as confirmed by Russo: 'It defines who you are as a business, how you operate and how you want to be perceived by those outside of your business. You really have to genuinely undertake, and go about your work, your engagement with your staff, your engagement with your clients in the way that you say you're going to from a culture perspective. You simply can't say our culture is *X* and define it, but then behave in a different way – *Y*. It's got to be really consistent.'

> *'Determine what behaviours and beliefs you value as a company, and have everyone live true to them. These behaviours and beliefs should be so essential to your core that you don't even think of it as culture.'* – **Brittany Forsyth**

Culture may be what attracts talent through the door, but what about retention? Remember that it's not your job to make people happy at work. If that's what you wish to do, go sell ice cream. Happiness is an inside job. Your role is to facilitate engagement and best performance out of people. A culture that breeds success, innovation and growth is also one that puts the people behind the project first. Adra's company Mossman adopts the same ideology – it's about building the people who build the projects. This ethos is starting to become the norm throughout the industry, as companies realise that the most valuable equity they have is their people.

Courtemanche reflects on Procore as it stands today: 'There's probably nothing more important. If you took the people out of it, there's not that much left, right? We have some technology, but when you put the people back in, it is the most special thing I've ever seen in my life. It's all about the people.' Culture is what informs your followership of what they can expect once they're part of your world. 'Once you hire them, you need people to feel like their thoughts are valued, their skills are put to use and that they are part of something that's bigger than themselves. That's where engagement comes in. It's about bringing the whole person to their job every single day. If we don't get that right, people just show up and punch the clock,' indicates Courtemanche. The old adage of people don't leave organisations, they leave people, has never been truer, especially in the social age when so much of leaders and organisations are on show.

Especially when you are working with individuals on a daily basis, you as a leader are always on show. Leaders attract a high level of visibility and taking responsibility for this is a key pillar of leadership as explained by Kurzydlo: 'Understand your responsibility as a role model in the business leader position. What I mean by that is understanding your responsibility, because people are always watching you, and they're making mental notes and subconscious deductions about your capacity as a leader. People are always looking to you for guidance, for faith and for understanding which way they should go. Always know that people are watching you.'

Nathan shared the story of when he was tasked with starting the Probuild branch in Sydney during the 2000s. Their ethos back then was 'hard but fair', with a master and commander type leadership style expected from the business leaders. There was also the simple rule that to work at Probuild meant a six-day work week. When Nathan started the business in Sydney, he found himself going into work every Saturday, when the office had no projects, only to shuffle papers and get ready for who to chase up on Monday. He realised there was no real vantage to this but knew that to change such a deep-rooted approach needed to start with him. 'I had to go on a transition as a person, as a leader in that business, to not work Saturdays. No-one will work Saturdays, because if I'm doing it then everyone else will do it out of the pressure. You see, a pillar of leadership owns the responsibility of being a role model. Not just as a good person or a good leader, but also to ensure that you are carrying those responsibilities of a business. They're watching you do so, and by doing that, they will understand themselves how to be a good leader in the future.'

It's important as a Triple E leader to have a hypersensitivity to culture, because a new alchemy of people, especially at the top, can illicit change, not always for the better. 'Sometimes changes in culture can never be pinpointed straight away, it happens over time, and culture shifts happen over time, but generally, more often than not, it happens from a business leader change, or a business leader coming in, or a new business leader having a dif-ferent way of doing things or shifting their approach at that top end – it has a ripple effect all the way through,' says Kurzydlo. 'It's interesting when you watch examples of where cultures have changed and why they've changed; it is all related to people. The people in those leadership roles are the ones that actually create the culture. Culture isn't something that can be bought or told. You can't generate culture quickly. It has to be created by the people in the business, in the leadership influential roles. The right leaders that have the right values, ethics, attitudes and approaches will be what creates the culture. That is the culture; it's as simple as that.' The education piece on why culture is important to a leader is imperative, because the culture of a project is a mirror of the leader. Not everyone comes ready-made, and even leaders who are influencing the culture should be given a chance to improve, but if they don't, '… That's when you need to make tough decisions as a business to potentially let a person go in those leadership influential roles. Not all businesses do it, especially when they're revenue sales-driving people but that is the hard decision and the right decision that needs to be made,' reflects Kurzyldo. As a Triple E leader, the project around you is your mirror of the culture you've created. So go back into your world tomorrow, and ask yourself, *Do I like what I see?*

GROWTH AND STRATEGY

'Mere change is not growth. Growth is the synthesis of change and continuity, and where there is no continuity there is no growth.' – **C S Lewis**

Growth requires a level of entrepreneurial cognition, but also a close investigation as to what is driving growth. This section pertains more to a business than a project but is necessary to highlight in the pursuit of Triple E leadership, because growth for growth's sake is never a sure-fire strategy for success, but there is an entrepreneurial leadership art form to construct a business to last fifty years rather than five years. And in the pursuit of making decisions that are best for business, leaders need to consciously assess growth and what that actually means for the business. Growth, like change, should never be implemented for the sake of it. Growth as a goal within itself is superficial, there needs to be the underlying value as to what it means, because there is no limit to it, especially in business. Growth can mean more opportunity to add more value to others and enable you to extend your impact further. What this really depends on is the type of service and value you are delivering to the market – there's a big difference if you're in the business of building towers or SaaS. Research in the *Journal of Management Studies* found that growth capabilities are an outcome of leadership behaviours and management activities combined, but growth doesn't simply mean growth in revenue. There can be a growth in revenue but a decline in profitability. Kurzydlo, who is in the business of growth, reflects that as a business leader, 'You are the one to actually make the decisions to assist in the company growth. You gather the data from the subject matter experts (SMEs). You then have the responsibility to make that decision for the company. Whilst other people will add value and suggest and make decisions along the way, when those hard decisions are made, it is your responsibility as a leader to make those decisions. You don't always have to make them, but in situations that require a decision that is tough to make, it is your responsibility to do so if others do not want to or cannot. Growth is important for people to realise that there are aspirations and visions and dreams for the company, but growth doesn't necessarily mean revenue. Growth can be within the sophistication of business processes, growth within how you do things, growth in innovation, growth in hiring different people to provide innovation. With the growth of these other things, growth in revenue will come as a by-product because of that.'

'Driving business growth is being able to analyse different ideas and then focus on the ones that you feel add the most value for your clients and yourselves as a business.'
– Sarah Slattery

In the book *Good to Great,* by Jim Collins, he introduces the hedgehog principle, which is premised on three pillars: 1. What you are deeply passionate about, 2. What you can be the best in the world at, and 3. What best drives your economic or resource engine. Businesses that were able to get from good to great constantly make great decisions in the confines of this concept, had a strategy to back up supreme execution and were able to beat the market for sustained periods of time. Kurzydlo agrees, stating that leaders need to, 'Understand what it is as a business you are doing and what is your point of difference, what it is you are providing and what it is you do differently to the market that will help drive that revenue growth.' Attracting growth is not about trying to fill every niche in the market or following the latest trends. It takes a high level of discipline to stick to a lane. In the same merit, be very clear as to why a business has reached a level that it needs to grow. Kurzydlo confirms, 'When you aim to do that, if it's revenue and growth for the sake of being big there needs to be more substance than that. There needs to be more substance as to what it is you're trying to achieve because otherwise it will fall over and won't be sustainable and you will not grow sustainably and effectively. If you're chasing money, you're going to try to do things potentially quicker and faster to get there, but that model has proven not to be sustainable in the past.' As a Triple E business leader, it's your duty to be very clear what growth actually means, what's the benefit to it and how the business wants to grow. There are businesses in the industry that have chased the shiny new objects (projects) and have rendered themselves to be out of business. It only takes one or two bad projects in the industry to sink a business.

I asked Rooney how a business leader can manage their niche, how they can be a hedgehog – doing the one thing that they're good at – while also taking into consideration opportunity in the marketplace. She commented, 'I think good strategy looks at where you'll be really effective and impactful. You'll sometimes see business leaders go through a phase where they'll scatter their resources too thin to the point where they actually can't drive change and impact. It comes down to knowing your values – your core value proposition – and ensuring that the ideas you're driving match that core value proposition and meet your customers' value proposition. A lot of people confuse capability and capacity. You can be capable but not have the short-term capacity. But growth does also mean identifying opportunities that still fall in your hedgehog zone, which is where strategy comes into play.'

When each contributor was asked what one of the most important functions was as business leader, there was total concurrence that setting the strategy was imperative. 'I think strategy is often oversold and under-imagined,' reflects Rooney.

For clarity, 'A vision is a great big idea of where you want to achieve, where you want to go, what you want to do. Strategy is how you're going to achieve that vision and what you have to do to get there, which sounds simple,' explains Kurzydlo.

Mirams adopted a very simple but highly effective strategy in the formation of Roberts Co; 'What we've tried to do, the business plan was formed by looking back through our careers of twenty and thirty years and saying, *What worked, repeat it – what didn't work, don't ever do that.* If you look at the issues in the construction industry, we have very high presenteeism, very high divorce rates and very high suicide rates. There is not a single bullet that fixes all of those things. It's the sum of a whole lot of low-hanging fruit that you need to attack simultaneously. When you start with a blank sheet of paper, we have been able to do that. What we said is let's get really great people. We have tried to leverage technology as best we can. We tried to build the company to be the most streamlined we could then put technology over the top and give people back their lives. We've been very conscious on saying, *We want you to have a life as well as a career*, and that we're not going to reward presenteeism – we're going to reward value.'

Part of growth and strategy is also having agility. This doesn't mean discarding what you are great at doing, for to succeed you need to pick one game and stick with it for a long period of time. But leadership is also about being able to identify when a specific course of action isn't working. For construction is certainly an industry where, on the ground, it's fast changing. Nathan gave an example of this. He spoke of a business leader in the industry that he worked with on an apartment project that, on the surface-level, seemed great at being able to run his company. But Nathan observed that he stuck too closely to his textbook practices and didn't take into consideration the nuances of a situation that was happening on the ground and in reality. He wouldn't sway from what he thought he knew, even with Nathan giving suggestions and ways of getting out of a difficult project. The inability to have agility and look at a situation practically resulted in the other contracting firm losing money on the project and caused extensive delays to the practical completion of the development. Nathan reflected on this subpar example of leadership, in which the business leader wasn't able to look outside of himself and recognise that there were better ways that the work could have been done. As a Triple E leader, you need to exercise situational awareness, or as Nathan says, reframe a situation.

Kurzydlo relays the same perspective: 'Be loose and malleable with your strategy. Your strategy doesn't have to be lineal; you can start the strategy and if it takes a different turn, be open to why and understand what that means. Maybe there's two different parts in how you're going to achieve that vision. I'd say continually assess your strategy, reassess, understand what you just started with and why it is changing.'

The best-kept plans, though, shouldn't be kept a secret within a business. Just as much as a vision needs to be constantly communicated, so does the strategy: 'More often than not, leaders forget to communicate the journey, the path and the travel to the business. There is a disconnect between the delivery of that, and then the vision upfront,' says Kurzydlo. I've been on all too many projects and just enough organisations to identify that there is an assumption that people within an organisation understand the strategy and also why it's being implemented. People need the road map and the reasoning in order to be part of implementing a strategy. Rooney reflects, 'When dealing with more senior audiences, particularly boards or external stakeholders, be aware that not everyone has exactly the same world view. Part of communicating the strategy is making sure that you give enough context for it to have meaning, depending on your stakeholders' backgrounds. It's like laying the breadcrumbs to Hansel and Gretel's house – joining the steps from where you are now to where you will be when your big idea is achieved.'

'Despair shows us the limit of our imagination. Imagination shared creates collaboration, and collaboration creates community, and community inspires social change.'
– Terry Tempest Williams

Inherently, by the nature of construction projects today, collaboration is required. No one single contractor has all the requirements in-house to deliver what they do. There can be just as many business functions that are fulfilled through collaboration. But collaboration is also a key to scaling on the business front. There are connotations that collaboration is cheating, because the only way to get ahead fast is just to do it all on your own. Take this book itself, for example. I could have written one without contribution, but the mission to raise the standards of leadership away from mediocrity will spread faster by collaboration. Collaboration is leverage and finding synergy where there are shared values and objectives. 'The greatest achievements of leaders are seldom made in isolation. Collaboration is the key,' notes Rooney. Collaboration is important, but certainly doesn't form 100% of a leadership function. 'Collaboration is important when you need to be collaborative,' says Nathan. The scale of collaboration, either on a macro or micro level will also be informed by the natural disposition of the leader, and above all, remaining authentic to your person is still at the core of any collaboration.

STAKEHOLDERS

'Do what you do so well that they will want to see it again and bring their friends.' – **Walt Disney**

Who is looking after your clients in such a way that they will become your raving fans and best advocates? It should be your business, and the people within. Before you think that I've put clients in a state of reverence, let's acknowledge that there are extremely difficult clients that, no matter what is done, it's never sufficient. That you could move heaven and earth, and they're still stuck in their ways, regardless of who you are or what you can do. One thing I will never do is compromise my own ethics, morality and sometimes sanity for a client. There are times when there is only so much you can do to assist and add value when a client won't even assist themselves. I once worked on a project where the client representative himself complained that he doesn't have time to read (not general literature – project correspondence). Now tell me, what do you do with that? That's the exemption, not the rule, so we'll proceed on the premise that most clients have a fair and reasonable modus operandi and don't wake up each morning thinking how to add stress and difficulty to a business they've engaged in service. For without clients, you're out of business. It's as simple as that. And Triple E leadership is about servicing your clients so they have an excellent *customer experience.*

I remember getting my first client under The Construction Coach. All of a sudden, I had this deep level of responsibility instilled into me. This person needed me and was enlisting a deep sense of trust for me to guide them to what they wanted to achieve. It was that moment which fixed within me how important it is to look after your clients as a business leader. Simple to say – it's best for business to look after your clients, but a whole different realm to actually do so. Caring about your client doesn't mean being their best friend and going out for lunch. It means caring about their problems enough and ensuring that the right course of action is taken to solve their problem. As Rooney confirms, 'Leaders should have their eyes on the customer – and want to make their life easier. The simplest way to do that is to ensure there's always a win-win for your partners. If you find yourself chasing a short-term outcome that suits your purposes, but won't meet their needs, then it probably will be a short-term relationship or short-term outcome, where you'll pay for it in the long-term. Take time to align. A key example for the Green Building Council is that we are being told sustainability has become too complex. A lot of our partners are finding it really hard to read the global land-scape. A lot of their teams are spending too long trying to stay up to date with rapidly accelerating change. That's why we've positioned ourselves to read the global tea leaves and to extract what's important for Australian property. Then we can create a ladder for the industry to climb. This approach becomes a genuine partnership where we lean in to invest resources and add value.'

'Always deliver more than expected.' – **Larry Page**

The first part of developing a deep partnership is to listen. Everyone is a prospective client, so when they come to you, it's not about you. It's about them. Rooney says, 'Leaders manage and partner with key stakeholders to learn what they want. Really listen to help people adapt.' Whatever the need of the client, they have a pain point and consideration that needs attention and resolution. What you think a client needs and what they actually need may be two completely different things. Impressing a solution onto a client that doesn't lead to mutually beneficial outcomes is a great disservice. Acting in the best interest of a client is imperative and a marker of Triple E leadership. At times, the client may not even know what is good for them, or right for them, but it's your duty to know that too and through your line of questioning, work to extract that. In order to serve your clients, you really need to get to know them. When I first meet clients, there are no assumptions. Assuming something about another party moves you into very dangerous territory. Take a minute to think why that actually is. Rooney provides insight into facilitating this deep partnership: 'Organisations that adapt well are the ones where the leaders listen, or they've set up mechanisms for listening in their organisations, whether they be regular reviews of customer feedback, poll surveys or website tracking. Essentially, what they're doing is listening, and making sure that their strategy remains on the right pathway. You can write your own strategy in isolation. But in a fast-moving area like sustainability, property or construction, you need to make sure that you're listening to the surroundings to check that there aren't nuanced changes to your direction.'

Nathan shared the example of the first response when the pandemic hit. 'Before we worried about ourselves, I wanted every single one of our staff to ring our clients. Not to talk about what we're doing or how we are, just say, *We're okay. What can we do for you? What issues do you have in your business at the moment?* I didn't care if it was in our fee or in our scope or if it's what we normally do – *What can we do to help you?* Flipping that kind of thinking, and saying, *Okay, well let's not be thinking of how bad it is for us, let's think about what we're going to do for our clients.* It just seemed like a natural approach after we rethought things. It was probably one of the best things.'

To best serve your clients, you need to know what it is that they value, as it isn't necessarily the same as what you value, and how your approach needs to consider the particulars and nuances of each client. It's the approach that Russo adopts: 'It's about building genuine relationships with your clients, knowing what it is that they need, what it is that they want to get from you as an industry expert and how to be best for that. What our offer to you as client A is going to be different to client B because every client has a slightly different need or want. Genuinely knowing your clients, what it is they need and what successful service delivery looks like is really important. If you, as a leader, don't understand that then it's really hard to expect successful outcomes.'

In the same instance as acting in the best interest of the business, you also need to act in the best interest of the client. Is the client always right? No, of course not. Clients are also people, and never let a job title be misconstrued for competency. Nathan shared the importance of maintaining truthfulness and integrity when faced with a particular direction from a client. The client was under pressure and needed his project team to fudge some numbers for cash flow and financing. It wasn't a lot of money, but Nathan made the call that there was another way to achieve the outcome without compromise. Sure, in the short-term a small movement of numbers may have been negligible, but it's out of alignment with values and also a disservice to the client. In construction, it's always advised to keep your nose clean because you do get found out – one way or another, things get flushed out. The easy thing in that situation would have been to comply, but the long-term implications would have compromised values and face. 'You can overcome a lot of problems by putting work in,' reflects Nathan. No-one ever loses out in the long-term if you act in the best interest of the client.

INNOVATION

'If I had asked people what they wanted they would have said faster horses.' – **Henry Ford**

Who is looking after your clients through service and product innovation if not you?

At the heart of thriving – not just surviving – is innovation. This enterprising trait of leaders has seen social, cultural, technological and policy innovations which have continuously cemented structural change in the industry. But innovation isn't valuable for innovation's sake – the same way that change isn't required for change's sake. Innovation is at the core of delivering greater value to your clients, community and market share than anything else, and what adds to position you as a Triple E leader. For example, my podcast, *Constructing You,* is an innovation, as is my book, this book, mentoring programs under my business, The Construction Coach, and even the content that is generated. Innovation can reflect an individual or a collective (project or organisation), and certainly isn't product-only based. But if you're not innovating and not delivering things of value to your clients, then someone else will, making them Triple E leaders and not you. In the book *Collective Genius: The Art and Practice of Leading Innovation,* the authors reflect on what most distinguishes innovative leadership. 'Truly innovative leaders are consistently able to elicit and then combine members' *separate slices of genius* into a single work of *collective genius*,' the authors write. Organisations today face dynamic environments with rapidly changing sentiments, requiring distinctive innovation to serve their clients and niche. Innovation is a real differentiator and marker of value, as it's not your degrees, certificates, rote advocacy or the like which will ever amount to Triple E leadership.

What matters just as much is the right type of leadership to drive and execute innovation with efficacy. A study done by the *Journal of Management and Organization* in 2018 found that innovative leaders can support organisational innovation by enhancing the motivation and ability of organisational members to be creative and innovative. Innovative leaders develop enthusiasm among organisational members to think out of the box, be more creative and to develop new ideas and solutions concerning organisational structures, processes and practices (Prasad and Junni, 2016). Take Mirams and the pioneering effort to introduce a five-day work week implemented on the Concord Hospital Redevelopment Project. Roberts Co and the NSW Government jointly engaged UNSW to study the benefits of the five-day work week on the mental health and wellbeing of site workers and their families. A year into the two-year construction phase, the research had already seen higher productivity and happiness onsite and an increase in quality of work and safety. Whether or not you agree with this move, as like any novel idea into a conservative marketplace is met with backlash, this is a boldly innovative move with tangible benefits for those concerned. 'What we're trying to do is if you look at the industry and see an issue, how do we solve it, not only for us but for the generations that will follow in our footsteps? That's really been the mantra, if you like, of what we've tried to do when we've established the company,' comments Mirams on the premise of building Roberts Co. It's an idea that no other tier one firm has introduced before. Many can talk all they desire about change, but few deliver on it, which is a strong trait of Triple E leaders. Innovation is about seeing a gap in the marketplace (opportunity) and creating new and unique solutions to fill the void. To generate solutions requires you to have distinctive thinking. For one, this is premised on not looking into the past to generate solutions for the future. It's 'blue ocean thinking', reflective of the blue ocean strategy which is concerned with differentiation and creating a captured demand in an uncontested marketplace. To innovate, you need to think. 'But most people would die sooner than think – in fact, they do,' said Bertrand Russell, British polymath.

A key to seeing innovation take place is patience. First, it needs to be embraced and encouraged, and that will be dictated by the culture or not, but second to that, patience is required. 'A good idea just needs time,' says Abraham, 'and sometimes the other thing is that a good idea looks amazing on paper. You can test it from every angle and every direction, and it is a flawless idea, but there may not be enough funding to go down that track at this particular point in time. Innovation must always have a place, but it can't take over what our core business is. It is not allowed to jeopardise or distract us from what our core business is every day, which is looking after our customers, giving them best quality outcome in the quickest possible time, and surviving as a business.' The introduction of anything new to a marketplace requires constant iteration, working through risks and building up the proof and recognition that this is now the status quo. And being the pioneers of anything new takes a lot of backbone. 'The pursuit of innovation can make us vulnerable to making mistakes with fatal consequences to our business. Bold, wise and definite leadership is required to navigate through the risks,' continues Abraham. When I was thinking about the opportunities in the industry for my business, The Construction Coach, I could have easily tacked on services that were parallel to what was already out there – technical and recognised professional training in which there was already a need for. Did I have an interest in providing construction management 101 training? No. But I did see that there was nothing that provided a holistic, inside out approach to career development in the industry, that had nothing to do with soft and fluffy training based on low-income and low-impact skill development and took into account the most influential factors on a person's career and life. I noticed that industry professionals and future leaders are working with outdated tools and practices, leaving behind massive opportunity on the table. So I introduced the new and novel mentoring and coaching that I do provide for the industry. The day that I conceived the idea wasn't the day that it was perfected, nor executed, nor refined so as to deliver unparalleled value and results to my clients. It simply took time, but had I not been patient and called it off too soon, then it would have been a total disservice to those it would be serving. When seeking to innovate, it comes down to the higher intelligence of a Triple E leader to know when to apply speed and when to apply patience. Having the two mixed up may not always lead to desired outcomes.

'Innovation distinguishes between a leader and a follower.'
– Steve Jobs

The second key to innovation is listening. As entrepreneurial-minded people, there may be a tendency to fall in love with our own solution because we're way too close to it. That's why trialling and testing, meshing and moulding are essential parts of the process. It can also be the greatest source of friction, but there is no excellence without it. 'You can have a great idea, but unless the marketplace and customers value what you sell, you're not going to go anywhere,' says Courtemanche. 'I would say you could never be too customer-focused, never be too close to the customer. When we're releasing new features and new product, and I have the customers telling us that they value what we've done – value it enough they want to pay for it, and it's actually going to improve their lives – you feel like you've de-risked it and that you're actually now able to deliver value and you feel confident in what you're doing. I know a lot of leaders and a lot of entrepreneurs can follow a path of passion around an idea that's not validated, and you can follow it too far. Of course, this isn't to say the client is always right.'

'If I had asked people what they wanted, they would have said faster horses,' said Henry Ford, American industrialist, business magnate and founder of Ford Motor Company. But you need to have your ears close to the ground. A great example of that is in 2017, Procore opened their first international office in Sydney. The team that was deployed after several months of being on the ground reflected that, unlike anything they've seen elsewhere, Australia and New Zealand have a real focus on safety and quality. Further market research allowed the team to realise the importance of that, and how legislation here enacted, supported and accelerated that. Procore, as a business, were able to hear what the collective community had to say, distilled that down into some products around quality and safety management that were well received and adopted.

Courtemanche reflects on the success as being, 'Generated from your markets and our ability just to listen to what you were telling us. I think the secret to innovation is distilling those ideas from great people's minds and making it into something that is valuable.' The key with listening is to be discerning, as what people want and what they actually need are typically two different things.

Innovation is a delicate art and science as well, for change for change's sake to simply demonstrate that something is happening doesn't yield long-term returns. Mirams explains, 'I love change when it's positive, and when we're making a difference, we're improving something. I don't change just for change's sake. When we're looking at something and saying, *How do we improve it? How do we make it more efficient? How do we make it better?* I find that really invigorating and I love it. I'm very comfortable in change, but I acknowledge not everyone is.' Approach innovation and change with an open mind and high discretion, and ensure that the due diligence has been thoroughly performed – for you might be the next mind that disrupts this industry. Instead of immediately thinking of all the ways it won't work, think about how you can make it work. I assure you the outcome will be significantly different.

LEAVING A LEGACY

'Carve your name on hearts not tombstones. A legacy is etched into the minds of others and the stories they share about you.'
– Shannon Adler

If people can be so lax and disrespectful of others' time, I don't want to know how they use and abuse their own. I have always been hypersensitive to time and how fleeting our human experience is. Time is one of my overarching values, and it dawns on me that one day I won't be here anymore. You won't. The people we all love won't. This isn't the dress rehearsal. This is the final act. The curtain isn't going to lift to give you another chance to do it all again. Do you know that the person who subscribes to mediocrity will be forgotten in less than one hundred years? Have you ever taken a moment to actually quantify how much of your waking time you really have to do all the things you want to be doing? It's not much at all. And within those waking years, you can only presume you'll be in excellent health come the last few decades so you can keep on doing what you want to be doing. Sure, the message may have been heard before, but just because you understand something on a superficial level still doesn't mean you embody the message. And what that looks like is most people wasting their life and their time like there is an abundance of it. But what if you want to add value to others even after you're gone? What if you want your name to be in the memories and stories of people once you have departed? You need to then build a legacy. You may not withstand the test of time but your value can. If you want to leave value behind even if you're not the person delivering it anymore, then it's time to get intentional with your legacy.

Legacy is the ability for others to carry on your work, your message and your organisation without you. Who is going to do that? And you need to ask yourself, *What do I need to start building today in order to achieve it?* The idea of my books, podcasts, programs and so many more things that I will continue to construct is with the ambition that they'll live on. And this is where construction can provide a false sense of legacy. John Maxwell quotes, 'It's not the buildings we build, but how well the people you invest in will carry on when you are gone.' There is a huge sense of pride and achievement that comes with leaving a construction project behind, but who will know that you worked on it? Unless your surname is the lead architect, the number of people who will know are slim. That was the founding impetus of *Constructing You,* which focuses on the people behind the projects, to start shifting the focus on the people who've had the vision. What kind of value do you need to add to the world for it to live on? I know that legacy isn't a high value for many, but before you reject the notion completely, spend some time with it. It may matter to you after all.

I asked Courtemanche what legacy he wishes to leave behind. In reflection, he responds saying, 'I want to have a positive impact on the lives that Procore touches; whether that's our employees, partners or customers. I want to create an environment where our employees truly thrive and to help them build skills that set them up for future success. I want to be a true partner to the construction industry, developing the platform that allows people to do the best work of their lives. Many of the structures the industry builds will outlast most of us, as will the impact they have on the communities that use them. The schools, hospitals and infrastructure of today all help contribute to a better future. We have the opportunity to leave behind a legacy where people got home safely from the jobsite, businesses grew and people loved their work.'

Legacy is closely tied with succession. I know that my mission and vision to drive change from the inside out of the construction industry won't be completed in my lifetime, nor can I alone reach all the people I would love to. That's why leaders develop other leaders, because they know that their impact will be greater and deeper if they do that. 'Growing other leaders from the ranks isn't just the duty of the leader, it's an obligation,' says Warren Bennis, American scholar and organisational consultant. If it's within your organisation, the investment in your leadership talent needs to happen sooner rather than later. If you've got an entrepreneurial streak, start that business. What kind of value do you need to start adding to the marketplace that ensures you live on in the hearts and minds of generations to come?

To start the conversation with yourself as to what legacy you wish to leave, sit with and think deeply on the following questions:

— If today was my last day on earth, what would I have wanted to achieve?
— If someone were to Google me in one hundred years, what would come up?
— What would I want my grandchildren's grandchildren to say about me?
— What problem do I want to take away from society, and when people are alleviated, it's because of me?
— If I were writing my own speech at my funeral, what would I want it to say and who would be reading it?

And on this existential note, we've come to the conclusion of the principles of Triple E leadership.

CONCLUSION

The synthesis of lessons, principles and wisdom generously shared by the contributors on *Constructing You*, and now this book, tied in with my own, are here to serve as your baseline and guidebook for Triple E leadership. Leadership is inherently complex, as you are dealing with the greatest variable of them all – people. This book was written to first give you the guiding principles and mental models, teamed with key insights into the leadership function, but at the highest standard. What most look for is a series of tactics when wanting to position themselves or demonstrate leadership capacity, but that only yields short-term success, if any, and surface-level impact and influence. You can just about include every topic and term under the umbrella of leadership, and if there was a prescription for leadership then it wouldn't be so rare and highly valued. The intention is for you to not stop developing your leadership curiosity – this book may have just ignited what is already within you, so you can go on your own exploratory journey of finding what leadership means to you, and how you can carry out that function to its highest value. You can only grow via pushing yourself, and that means taking the lessons from this book into your own real-time application.

But there is still one qualification required to you becoming a Triple E leader. And it's to take immediate and massive action to set yourself on that path. There is no antidote to doing, and no way to pass the sweat equity required to construct something brilliant out of yourself, others or projects. You can read about eating healthy until the end of time, but until you do, nothing changes. You can read about running – what's the best shoe to get, where's the best track to run, how long you should run – but nothing will change until you actually go out there and run. It's the same with leadership. All the leadership literature in the world cannot replace the doing part, being on the cold front day in and day out and living all of your life in accordance with higher standards. Until you do not cut the cord with your comfort zone, I assure you nothing magnificent or significant will or can change.

The thing with opportunity is that the door closes on it. It will not be waiting around for you to be ready, to find the right time, to have everything in order and then – only then – do you start. Opportunity is fleeting, and every day that passes, think of it as sand flowing through an hourglass. You need to deeply consider, *When will I make a start?* Because if you think being a Triple E leader with lasting impact for who you are and what you know takes months, you'll be sorely mistaken. It takes years, decades, a lifetime, and that's even if you know all of what you need to do and when. It takes more time than you can imagine, and I know this very well. What doesn't have an expiry are your excuses. They can be around with you until the end of time. If you don't start today, by taking immediate and massive action, you also aren't allowing one of the most beautiful principles of mankind to kick in: compounding. The return on investment on zero will always be zero.

If you've read this far into the book, then you have presented yourself at a crossroad. You can continue doing as you were doing, missing out on a significant world of opportunity not just for yourself but for others, and go back to life as it was. Or, you can choose excellence; you can choose to walk down the path less travelled, and be the disruptor that the construction industry so vehemently needs – the Triple E leader. If you choose the latter, I look forward to seeing you win. The only way onwards and upwards is to start leading.

Until the next book, I want to see you win – here's to Constructing You.

ACKNOWLEDGEMENTS

To the nine exemplary leaders and industry titans who have extended the generosity of their time and contributed their insights, advice and lessons learnt over decades-long careers, I thank you each for your belief and support of the mission of this book: Alison Mirams, David Russo, Davina Rooney, George Abraham, Mark Nathan, Melanie Kurzydlo, Rami Adra, Sarah Slattery and Tooey Courtemanche.

I wouldn't be writing this book if it wasn't for the first ten guests who said yes for my podcast. I started approaching some industry titans in late December 2019. I remember staring at the message on LinkedIn thinking, *If I press it, I know I'm setting into motion something big and ambitious ... and I'd love them to say yes.* Getting the first yeses from people that I have both only interacted with online or have never spoken to at all served as immense fuel and confirmation to keep on going. Thank you to all the guests, past and future on *Constructing You* who have shared invaluable insights that will continue to serve the industry for decades to come.

Dad, there is nothing in this world that I know you wouldn't do for me, and for that I love you more that words can say. It is your lessons, which have guided you for decades, that you have consistently pressed into me that have made me much of the person I am today. The leader that is within me is very much a reflection of you, as we happen to be copies of each other. For you have taught me some of the most important principles and philosophies for life that have continued to serve me and will until the end of time.

Mum, thank you for sacrificing all that you possibly can so that I have every opportunity possible to achieve whatever it is I want. I love the awe that you have of me, the constant support and how proud you are of my every move. It's my duty to make you proud, for all that you have poured into our family shall never be in vain. You are a leader in our little family, always steering us towards a home that has love, comfort and happiness in it.

Leadership was a notion that I had reserved for myself after decades of experience thinking this was reserved for some limited upper echelon of society. Thank you to my mentor, confidante and exemplary leader, Ron Malhotra, for letting me write an alternative future for myself. Thank you for reaching out into it and pulling it all forward for me so I get to do what I do, be who I am and have what I have. Until the end of time, I will be grateful and moved all over again that I get to stand on your shoulders and know you in this lifetime. You are larger than life itself and the epitome of living life to the highest standards. Thank you to Caroline Vass, for believing in every breath of my vision from the first moment that I spoke it into existence. You are unparalleled in your leadership, and it is something to be revered and aspired to, and your power and ability is larger than life too. There is no constructing me or others if it wasn't for you both. I appreciate you both until the end of time for holding up the mirror so I can see clearly and enabling me to be more, do more and have more, as you do to so many others around the world.

The last few years have been enlightening, to say the least, and I give my daily gratitude to the supreme creator and master of the universe, for bestowing on me the duty and ability to lead. It's a divine purpose to be granted that I have the duty of upholding. Thank you for always having my back and allowing things to turn out better than even I ever could have expected.

I remember the first few messages I received and was curiously waiting for on the release of my podcast. Every message is met with deep appreciation; for it is solely for you that I drive and strive to keep on delivering my podcast. Thank you to those who have made *Constructing You* part of your daily walks, Sunday morning breakfasts and weekend binge listens, and your auditory brilliance on the drive to work. Thank you to each constructor for choosing to come on this journey to construct yourself with me and your exceptional future. We're going to go fast and far. You ready?

Ready to become an impactful and influential industry leader?
Start your journey at theconstructioncoach.com.au

ABOUT THE AUTHOR

Elinor Moshe is an ambitious and driven Thought Leader, bestselling author, podcast host and businesswoman disrupting the construction industry. She's the founder of The Construction Coach; Australia's first construction coach. As the podcast host of *Constructing You,* Elinor interviews exemplary leaders and industry titans who dominate construction business and careers. She is the bestselling author of a one-of-a-kind book, *Constructing Your Career.* She ties her distinctive thinking and uncommon insights with over eight years' experience in the commercial construction industry, to generate transformative and exceptional results for her clients. Elinor has been featured by *Entrepreneur Asia Pacific, Passion Vista* as a 2021 Woman Leader to Look Up To, in *Yahoo! Finance, Australian National Construction Review* and over forty global podcasts discussing her career, leadership and business acumen. She holds a Master of Construction Management and Bachelor of Environments from the University of Melbourne. Her passion is to construct exceptional futures, and that starts with constructing *you.* Elinor lives in Melbourne, Australia.

www.ingramcontent.com/pod-product-compliance
Lightning Source LLC
Chambersburg PA
CBHW021431180326
41458CB00001B/219